550
AIR FRYER
RECIPES
COOKBOOK

Easy, Delicious & Foolproof Air Fryer Recipes Anyone Can Make for Healthy Living
BY
Francis Michael

ISBN: 978-1-952504-31-0

DISCLAIMER

The information contained in this book is geared for educational and entertainment purposes only. Concerted efforts have been made towards providing accurate, up to date and reliable complete information. The information in this book is true and complete to the best of our knowledge.

Neither the publisher nor the author takes any responsibility for any possible consequences of reading or enjoying the recipes in this book. The author and publisher disclaim any liability in connection with the use of information contained in this book. Under no circumstance will any legal responsibility or blame be apportioned against the author or publisher for any reparation, damages, or monetary loss due to the information herein, either directly or indirectly.

Table of Contents

AIR FRYER BEEF & PORK RECIPES 82

AIR FRYER MAIN MEAL RECIPES

AIR FRYER EGG RECIPES

AIR FRYER SIDE DISH RECIPES 129

AIR FRYER VEGAN & VEGETARIAN RECIPES 141

AIR FRYER BURGER RECIPES 152

AIR FRYER APPETIZER RECIPES 163

AIR FRYER DESSERT RECIPES 174

INTRODUCTION

Benefits of Cooking With an Air Fryer

It is pertinent to know what an Air Fryer is before knowing what you can benefit from the Air Fryer. An Air Fryer is kitchen equipment programmed to use oil or sometimes hot air which moves around the food to aid proper cooking of the food.

Although there are other cooking methods but Air Fryer gives a lot of benefits. The benefits are listed below:

1. **Easy to Use:**

The unit does not require much settings before you start cooking. You just need to choose the temperature and frying time, place the food and shake the basket about 2 or 3 times before cooking time is completed.

Shaking the basket helps the food to be properly cooked. When you open the appliance, it does not lose lots of heat.

2. **Saves Space:**

This particular benefit is what those who live in a small apartment really appreciate. The size of the appliance is appreciative because it does not consume a big space and it is easy to store.

It is small, handy to carry and can replace unit like toaster oven. One who has an office break room can comfortably keep this appliance there.

3. **Efficient in Energy:**

Using an Air Fryer has energy efficiency compared to using a microwave oven. It does not heat up your house unnecessarily. If you use this appliance to cook, be assured that your kitchen would not be too hot. This gives an impressive motive for you to use the unit for cooking.

4. **Quicker Meals:**

This appliance is programmed with a device that enables it to cook food at a faster rate. Although they are smaller in size than an oven but they cook food faster and it can take about 8 – 10 minutes to preheat.

This may differ if you are using a microwave oven. A normal microwave oven may take up to 40 or 45 minutes to perfectly cook frozen fries but Air Fryer could take about 15 minutes. This show how fast and unique is the appliance.

5. **Gives Healthier Cooking:**

This is very easy. The equipment can cook a healthy food with or without oil if you desire. Example of foods that can be cooked with this appliance includes: onion rings, frozen fries, wings and more. They can be cooked without any extra oil. It gives a crispy and impressive cooking.

6. **Easy to Clean:**

Sometimes cleaning up a cooking machine is boring and some people feel reluctant to clean the unit immediately after use because of many parts that needs to be clean up.

You only have to clean the Air Fryer basket and pan. Other parts are dishwasher-safe. Cleaning up those two parts after use takes just few minutes.

7. **It is Versatile:**

Much can be done with this appliance. Its versatility is one of the Air Fryer's unique features that enable food to be fried properly. The Air Fryer can also be used to boil, roast, and bake etc.

The appliance also helps to warm leftovers, cook frozen and fresh foods. Some features that you would find in the Air Fryer include cooking rack, grill pan, rotisserie rack and cooking basket etc. The cooking basket can allow you to cook many things at the same time.

How the Air Fryer Works

It is important to have a pre-knowledge about the Air Fryer and how it works. What you need to know is that the Air Fryer works by putting oil to fully coat your food while the air that is going round heats the Air Fryer up to 400°F. The appliance uses less oil to fry compared to other fryers. The unit can fry foods like fish, steak, potato chips and French fries etc. The appliance is programmed to use an adjustable temperature and cooking time. The basket in which the food is placed has to be shaken from time to time to make a proper cooking. However, there are some models that perform this task automatically.

How to Use an Air Fryer

1. **Spray food with cooking spray**:
You are required to spray your food with cooking spray or oil to allow the food not to stick on the Air Fryer basket. Little oil is required.

2. **Avoid overcrowding:**
The unit uses air to circulate air around the food; it does not need the food to be overcrowded. Allow enough space to enable proper air circulation for your cooking to be crispy.

3. **Shake the basket:**
When you start cooking, make sure to shake the Air Fryer basket. Shake the basket about 2 times before the cooking time completes at an interval of 5 minutes. This ensures a proper cooking.

4. **Keep the unit dry:**
If you are cooking marinating food, be sure to pat dry the food before cooking so that there will not be excessive smoke. If you are cooking foods like chicken wings, remove the fat from the bottom of the Air Fryer from time to time.

How to Clean an Air Fryer

1. **Unplug the appliance:**
Make sure the appliance is not still connected to any power source before you start cleaning the appliance. Remove the appliance from any power source, turn it off and allow it to cool for about 25 – 30 minutes.

2. **Wipe the heating element:**
Doing this requires you to keep the unit upside down and wipe the heating element with a sponge.

3. **Wipe both the inside and outside:**
Use sponge and warm water to wipe the inside of the unit while for the outside, dip a cotton cloth into and wipe the unit.

4. **Remove any food residue:**
Be sure to get rid of stuck up food residue both inside and outside of the unit. You can use a baking soda, prepare a paste and wipe any place you find any food residue using sponge and then dry it with any cloth that is made of cotton.

5. **Clean the cooking basket and the pan:**
Air Fryer cooking basket and pan are very easy to wash. The task of washing them is not too demanding and as such requires a simple washing method. However, there exist some Air Fryer models that both the cooking basket and the pan are dishwasher safe. You just have to use a sponge and warm soapy water.

6. **Soak the cooking pan and the basket:**
Soaking the cooking pan and the basket is necessary when you have hard food residue on both the pan and cooking basket. Put the basket in the pan and soak with warm water for about 8-10 minutes. Finally clean with sponge.

7. **Air-dry all the parts:**
After a proper cleaning, the entire appliance will be soaked with water. You may use a cotton cloth to dry the parts or you keep them for some hours to naturally dry.

How to Maintain Your Air Fryer

The longevity of the appliance lies on the proper maintenance of the equipment. Improper maintenance will lead to total damage or malfunctioning of the appliance. The maintenance tips are listed below:

1. Before you start using the appliance, check for any debris and remove it. An Air Fryer that stays for a longer time without being used may has some dust inside the unit. You have to check the inside and clean the dust if found any. Check the pan and cooking basket for dust or food residue and then clean properly and start using.

2. Make sure to inspect the cords before use. This does not really mean just plugging the cords but to check if the cord is damaged or has any cut on it as a faulty cord could cause you an injury. After inspecting the cord and found no fault, you can start using the appliance.

3. Proper placement of the appliance is required. Keep it upright on a flat surface.

4. There are some foods that require you to cook in batches depending on the size of your Air Fryer; you can start cleaning the unit after the last batch is fully cooked.

5. Check each part, for example cooking basket, handle or pan before use. Get any faulty parts direct from the manufacturer if you found any.

6. Make sure you store the appliance in an upright position and do not fail to remove the cord from the wall or any power source. Safe-keep the cords so that they do not quickly damaged.

7. Do not keep the unit close to another unit or a wall. For proper circulation of hot air, the Air Fryer requires a minimum space of about 4 inches behind and above them for a proper functioning of the appliance while cooking. Make sure the air fryer is not placed close to a wall or another appliance.

Air Fryer Frequently Asked Questions and Answers

1. **What is an air fryer?**

As earlier said before, an Air Fryer is kitchen equipment programmed to use oil or sometimes hot air which moves around the food to aid proper cooking of the food. Some people think as the name implies "Air Fryer" that it is a fryer. Definitely it is not a fryer rather an appliance that cooks food by circulating hot air around the food. This process is well known as convection because it uses less oil. The appliance also allows you to cook other foods.

2. **Is air frying healthier than deep frying?**

Foods that have plenty of oil are not good for consumption. Air Fryer makes use of less oil. The Air Fryer gives you a crispy result on foods like chicken, fish, French fries and many others. It is tested and recommended that Air-fried foods taste better than food cooked with a microwave oven.

3. **Do I need to preheat the air fryer before cooking?**

In most cases you do not need to preheat your Air Fryer before you start cooking. Compared to a traditional oven, Air Fryer heats at a faster rate more than the traditional oven. Another interesting fact about the Air Fryer is that the total cook time starts when the Air Fryer is still cold.

4. **How much food can an Air Fryer hold?**

This depends on the particular food. Some Air Fryers can contain food for 4 servings. When the food is much, it is advisable to cook in batches to avoid overcrowding the food on the Air Fryer basket. If all the food can fit into the Air Fryer basket at the same time without overcrowding, you can cook all at the same time.

5. **Do I need to purchase extra components and attachments for my Air Fryer?**

Air Fryers are manufactured with components or attachments which include: cooking pans and rack. For the purpose of this manual, we mostly make use of the Air Fryer cooking basket.

6. **In what way can I prevent food from sticking to my Air Fryer?**

It is possible for food to stick into the Air Fryer basket while cooking. Foods like breaded chicken or fish can stick into your cooking pan. You have to sprinkle oil on the pan before cooking.

7. **In what way can I clean my Air Fryer?**

It is pertinent to clean the Air Fryer after use. Component like the cooking basket in some models are dishwasher-safe. You need to periodically clean the main body of your Air Fryer to avoid smoking which could be caused by grease and food splatters. After cooking, allow the appliance to cool for about 10-15 minutes. Do not fail to allow it dry after cleaning.

8. **What must I do if smoke comes out while Air Frying? Or brings out unusual smell?**

This might be as a result of irregular cleaning of your Air Fryer. Generally, if you experience this problem, then it means that your Air Fryer is dirty because it is the debris that will bring out the smell or smoke. Clean the area surrounding the heating element.

AIR FRYER BREAKFAST RECIPES

Breakfast Frittata

Preparation Time: 15 minutes
Cook Time: 20 minutes
Total Time: 35 minutes

Ingredients:

- Cooking spray
- ½ Cup shredded Cheddar-Monterey Jack cheese blend
- 2 Tbsp. red bell pepper, diced
- 1 Green onion, chopped
- ¼ Lbs. breakfast sausage, fully cooked and crumbled
- 4 Eggs, lightly beaten
- 1 Pinch cayenne pepper (optional)

Cooking Instructions:

1. In a small mixing bowl, mix together bell pepper, sausage, eggs, onion, Cheddar-Monterey Jack cheese, and cayenne.
2. Preheat the Air Fryer to 360°F. Sprinkle cooking spray on a non-stick cake pan.
3. Put the prepared egg mixture into the cake pan.
4. Put them into the Air-fryer and Air-fry for 20 minutes.
5. Serve and enjoy!!!

Breakfast Egg Rolls

Preparation Time: 10 minutes
Cook Time: 8 minutes
Total Time: 18 minutes
Serves: 12

Ingredients:

- 8 Strips bacon, cooked and cut into pieces
- 1 Tbsp. hot sauce (Sriracha)
- ½ Cup maple syrup
- 1 Cup shredded cheese
- 12 Egg roll wrappers
- 6 Eggs, scrambled
- 3 Cups frozen hash browned, browned in a skillet
- ½ Cup ketchup

Cooking Instructions:

1. Boil the eggs and allow it to cool. In a skillet, brown the hash browns. Crisp the bacon in a skillet and chop into small sizes.
2. Fill each wrapper with small portion of the filling ingredients. To make the wrapper stick, brush the edges with small water.
3. Roll the egg rolls and keep them at one Conner.
4. Put about 2 inches of vegetable oil and heat the skillet.
5. In batches, fry the egg rolls. After sometimes, turn over and fry both sides again.
6. Flip onto a serving plate. Top with maple syrup.
7. Serve and enjoy!!!

French toast Bites

Preparation Time: 10 minutes
Cook Time: 15 minutes
Total Time: 25 minutes
Serves: 8

Ingredients:

- cinnamon
- milk and almond milk (optional)
- 4 pieces of bread
- 3 eggs
- sugar

Cooking Instructions:

1. Preheat your Air Fryer at 360°F for about 5 minutes.
2. Whisk together 3 eggs in a small bowl.
3. Combine together cinnamon and 1/3 cup sugar in a small bowl.
4. Cut 4 pieces of bread into two, make them in ball shape.
5. Soak the bread into the egg mixture.
6. Put the bread into cinnamon mixture.
7. Put all the balls in Air Fryer and bake at 360°F for 15 minutes.
8. Serve and enjoy!!!

Bacon Wrapped Mini Breakfast Burritos

Preparation Time: 10 minutes
Cook Time: 25 minutes
Total Time: 35 minutes
Serves: 4
Ingredients:
- 2 Tbsp. cashew butter
- 3 Tbsp. tamari
- 2 Tbsp. liquid smoke
- 2 Tbsp. water
- 4 Pieces rice paper
- 2 servings Vegan Egg scramble

Veggie Toppings:
- ⅓ cup roasted sweet potato cubes
- 8 strips roasted red pepper
- 1 small tree broccoli, sautéed
- 6-8 stalks fresh asparagus
- handful spinach, kale, other greens

Cooking Instructions:
1. Preheat oven to 350°F and place the baking sheet with parchment.
2. Whisk together tamari, cashew butter, liquid smoke and water in a small bowl. Make all the fillings and gather the rolls.
3. For rice paper hydration, get a big bowl and hold one rice paper under cool water to wet both side of the wrapper for about 10 seconds.
4. Remove from water and flip onto a plate.
5. Put the ingredients on the middle of the rice paper and fold two sides in a form of burrito. Bury each roll into cashew - liquid smoke mixture and align them on a baking sheet.
6. Air-fry at 350°F for 15 minutes. After sometimes, turn over and Air-fry both sides for another 10 minutes.
7. Serve and enjoy!!!

Monte Cristo Sandwich

Preparation Time: 10 minutes
Cook Time: 18 minutes
Total Time: 28 minutes
Serves: 12

Ingredients:

- 1 Egg
- 3 Tbsp. half and half
- 2½ Oz. sliced Swiss cheese
- 2 Oz. slices deli ham
- ¼ Tsp. vanilla extract
- Powdered sugar
- Raspberry jam
- 2 Slices sourdough, white or multigrain bread
- 2 Oz. sliced deli turkey
- 1 Tsp. butter, melted

Cooking Instructions:

1. In a small mixing bowl, mix together vanilla, egg and half and half.
2. Set a place on the counter and keep the bread. Prepare a sandwich using a slice of ham, Swiss cheese and turkey.
3. Add the second slice of Swiss cheese on one side of the bread. Preheat the Air Fryer to 350°F.
4. Cut an aluminium foil to the size of the bread and spray melted butter on the foil. Put the sandwich into the egg mixture for about 25 seconds on each side.
5. Put the sandwich on the aluminium foil and turn it to the Air Fryer basket. Air-fry at 350°F for 10 minutes.
6. After sometimes, turn over and Air Fry both sides for another 8 minutes. Flip onto a serving and sprinkle with powdered sugar. Top with raspberry.
7. Serve and enjoy!!!

Loaded Cauliflower Hash-browns

Preparation Time: 10 minutes
Cook Time: 10 minutes
Total Time: 28 minutes
Serves: 4
Ingredients:

- 1 Egg

- ½ Cup of chickpea, almond, or all-purpose flour
- 1 Head of cauliflower
- ½ Cup of finely diced onion
- 1 Cup of grated Cheddar cheese
- ½ Tsp. paprika
- 4 Slices thick-cut bacon, diced
- ½ Cup of finely diced red and green bell pepper
- 1 Tsp. salt

Freshly ground pepper to taste

Cooking Instructions:
1. Pre-heat the Air Fryer to 400°F. Air-fry the onions and bacon for 10 minutes.
2. Nicely chop your cauliflower in a food processor. Put the cauliflower into a kitchen towel and squeeze all the water out.
3. Put the cauliflower in a large mixing bowl and put the egg, flour, bacon, onions, peppers, Cheddar cheese, salt and paprika.
4. Stir thoroughly. Create about 8 oval shape patties and put in a freezer for about an hour. Preheat Air Fryer to 400°F with small oil.
5. Air-fry the hash browns in batches for 10 about minutes. Season with salt and freshly ground black pepper. After sometimes, turn over and Air Fry both sides.
6. Serve and enjoy!!!

Deep Dish Prosciutto, Spinach and Mushroom Pizza

Preparation Time: 20 minutes
Cook Time: 35 minutes
Total Time: 55 minutes
Serves: 2

Ingredients:

- ¼ Tsp. Italian seasoning
- 12 Oz. pizza dough
- ⅓ Cup of pizza sauce
- 1½ Cups of grated mozzarella cheese
- 3 Oz. thinly sliced prosciutto
- 3 Oz. button mushrooms, sliced
- ½ Cup of frozen spinach, thawed
- 1 Tbsp. olive oil

Cooking Instructions

1. Toss the mushrooms with the Italian seasoning and olive oil. Set aside. Squeeze liquid out from the spinach and set aside.
2. Preheat Air Fryer to 370°F. Lubricate the baking pan with olive oil. Make the pizza dough into a circle of about 8 inches in diameter and flip them into the pan.
3. With a fork, Dig the dough by making holes in the bottom crust and flip them to the Air Fryer basket. Air-fry at 370°F for 5 minutes.
4. Remove the pan from the air fryer. Turn the crust onto a plate, shake them and return it back into the pan. Put the pan back on the Air Fryer and air-fry for 5 minutes.
5. Put sauce into the pizza and top with half of the mozzarella cheese. Put mushroom and half of the spinach over the cheese in layers.
6. Chop the prosciutto into fine pieces and put them on top of the pizza. Air-fry at 350°F for about 11 minutes.
7. Serve and enjoy!!!

White Bean Toasts With Burst Grape Tomatoes and Pancetta

Preparation Time: 10 minutes
Cook Time: 20 minutes
Total Time: 30 minutes
Serves: 4

Ingredients:

- 8 Oz. pancetta
- 1 Cup of grape tomatoes
- 1 Can of cannellini beans, drained and rinsed
- 2 Tbsp. olive oil
- 1 Tbsp. chopped fresh rosemary
- Salt and freshly ground black pepper
- 4 Slices of thick-sliced Ciabatta bread
- Chopped fresh chives

Cooking Instructions:

1. Pre-heat the Air Fryer to 400°F. Chop pancetta into ½-inch cubes and flip them into the Air Fryer basket.
2. Air-fry at 400°F for 8 minutes. Shake the Air Fryer basket and launch in the grape tomatoes. Air-fry for another 7 minutes.
3. Keep the pancetta and tomatoes aside. Put olive oil and the cannellini beans into a big bowl. Use the back of a fork to break the beans until they are properly crushed.
4. Sprinkle rosemary, salt and ground black pepper to taste. Grease the bread slices with olive oil and put them in the Air Fryer.
5. Air-fry at 400°F for 5 minutes. Fry both sides for even browning. Gather the toasts by spreading crushed cannellini bean mixture on each of the toasted slice.
6. Top with tomatoes and some pancetta season with freshly ground black pepper.
7. Serve and enjoy!!!

Perfect Cinnamon Toast

Preparation Time: 5 minutes
Cook Time: 5 minutes
Total Time: 10 minutes
Servings: 6

Ingredients:

- ½ Cup of White Sugar
- 1 ½ Tsp. Ground Cinnamon
- 1 ½ Tsp. Pure Vanilla Extract
- 12 Slices Bread whole wheat is great
- 1 Stick Salted Butter room temperature
- 6 Cranks of Fresh Ground Black Pepper

Cooking Instructions:

1. Mash softened butter with a back of spoon and put vanilla, sugar, cinnamon, and pepper. Stir thoroughly.
2. Dip bread into the mixture.
3. Put the number of slices that can enter your Air Fryer.
4. Cook at 400°F for 5 minutes. Pick from Air Fryer and chop nicely.
5. Serve and enjoy!!!

Tofu Scramble

Preparation Time: 5 minutes
Cook Time: 30 minutes
Total Time: 35 minutes
Servings: 3
Calories: 409kcal

Ingredients:

- ½ Tsp. garlic powder
- ½ Tsp. onion powder
- ½ Cup of chopped onion
- 2 ½ Cups of chopped red potato
- 1 Block tofu - chopped into 1" pieces
- 2 Tbsp. soy sauce
- 1 Tbsp. olive oil
- 1Tsp. turmeric
- 1 Tbsp. olive oil
- 4 Cups of broccoli florets

Cooking Instructions:

1. Mix together the soy sauce, tofu, olive oil, onion, turmeric, garlic and onion powder in a medium mixing bowl.
2. In another different small mixing bowl, put the potatoes in the olive oil and air fry at 400°F for 15 minutes.
3. After about 7 minutes, turn over and Air Fry both sides. Put the tofu and potatoes into Air Fryer and Air-fry at 370°F for another 15 minutes.
4. When it is about 5 minutes remaining on the cook time, put the broccoli into Air Fryer.
5. Serve and enjoy!!!

Breakfast Sausage Wraps

Preparation Time: 5 minutes
Cook Time: 6 minutes
Total Time: 11 minutes
Serves: 3

Ingredients:
- 1 Can of 8 count Refrigerated Crescent Roll Dough
- Syrup, Ketchup or BBQ
- 8 Wooden Skewers
- 8 Heat N' Serve Sausages
- 2 Pieces American Cheese cut into ¼

Cooking Instructions:
1. Select the Crescent Rolls and keep them on a flat surface.
2. Open Sausages and cut Cheese.
3. Carefully keep One Crescent Roll on the flat surface unrolled. Make a triangle from the roll working from Wide triangle to tip of the triangle.
4. Put cheese strip and sausage to the largest part of the crescent roll.
5. Roll the dough to the tip of the triangle and put about 4 of the rolls into your Air Fryer.
6. Air-fry at 380°F for 3 minutes. Flip onto a serving plate and put skewer. Top with BBQ, syrup or ketchup.
7. Serve and enjoy!!!

Greasy Spoon Home Fried Potatoes

Preparation Time: 30 Minutes
Cook Time: 35 minutes
Total Time: 1 hour 5 minutes
Serves: 4

Ingredients:

- 3 Large Potatoes scrubbed and diced into cubes
- 1 Medium Yellow and Brown Onion diced
- 1 Small Red Pepper diced
- 2 Tbsp. Bacon Grease
- 2 Tsp. Sea Salt
- 1 Tsp. Onion Powder
- 1 Tsp. Garlic Powder
- 1 Tsp. Paprika

Cooking Instructions:

1. Put the potatoes into a big bowl and soak with water for 30 minutes.
2. Combine together all seasonings and keep aside. Lubricate your Air Fryer Basket with Coconut Oil.
3. Strain potatoes, dry it well and place into a big mixing bowl. Put Bacon Grease or Oil to your potatoes and combine them. Put potatoes into Air Fryer Basket.
4. Cook potatoes at 370°F for 20 minutes, shake while cooking. Cut Red peppers and onions and put into the mixing bowl and keep aside.
5. Flip potatoes into bowl with peppers and onions and combine. Put seasonings and combine. Put mixture into Air Fryer Basket and finally into the Air Fryer.
6. Cook at 380°F for 10 more minutes.
7. Serve and enjoy!!!

Breakfast Hash Browns

Preparation Time: 15 minutes
Cook Time: 15 minutes
Total Time: 30 minutes
Serves: 8

Ingredients:

- 2 Tsp. Chili flakes
- 1 Tsp. Garlic powder
- 1 Tsp. Onion Powder
- 4 Peeled and finely grated Large potatoes
- 2 Tbsp. Corn flour
- Salt to taste
- Pepper powder to taste
- 2 Tsp. Vegetable Oil

Cooking Instructions:

1. Cover the grated potatoes with water and allow it to soak. Strain the water to remove excess starch from the potatoes.
2. Heat 1 Tsp. vegetable oil in a non-stick pan and sauté shredded potatoes till cooked slightly for 4 mins.
3. Allow to cool and flip the potatoes to a plate. Put salt, pepper, garlic, onion powder, corn flour, chili flakes and combine together thoroughly.
4. Spread over the plate and pat it firmly with your fingers. Keep in a refrigerator for 20 minutes.
5. Preheat Air Fryer at 180ºC. Remove the refrigerated potato and chop into equal sizes.
6. Grease the Air Fryer basket with oil, Put the hash brown pieces into the basket and fry for 15 minutes at 180ºC.
7. Remove the basket and turn the hash browns at 6 minutes to the other side.
8. Serve and enjoy!!!

French toast Sticks

Preparation Time: 5 minutes
Cook Time: 12 minutes
Total Time: 17 minutes
Serve: 4

Ingredients:

- Cinnamon
- Nutmeg
- Ground cloves
- 4 Pieces of sliced bread
- 2 Tbsp. soft butter
- 2 Eggs gently beaten
- Salt
- Icing sugar and maple syrup

Cooking Instructions:

1. Preheat Air Fryer to 180ºC.
2. Gently beat together two eggs, cinnamon, salt, and small amount of nutmeg and ground cloves in a bowl.
3. Spread butter on both sides of the sliced breads and chop into strips.
4. Coat each strip in the egg mixture and arrange them in Air Fryer.
5. Pause the Air Fryer and remove the pan after 2 minutes of cooking. Spray the bread with cooking spray.
6. After dredging the strips thoroughly, flip and spray the second side too.
7. Place pan back on fryer and cook for 4 more minutes, monitor while cooking to avoid burning.
8. Remove from Air Fryer and garnish with icing sugar and maple syrup.
9. Serve and enjoy!!!

Air Fryer Donuts

Preparation Time: 10 minutes
Cook Time: 8 minutes
Total Time: 18 minutes
Serve: 4

Ingredients:

- 1 Tsp. cinnamon
- 4 Tbsp. dark brown sugar
- Pinch of allspice
- 1 Can of Pillsbury Grands Flaky Layers biscuits
- 3 Tbsp. melted butter
- 1/3 Cup granulated sugar

Cooking Instruction:

1. Mix brown sugar, allspice sugar, and cinnamon, in a small bowl and keep aside.
2. Remove the biscuits from can and cut the holes out of the center of each biscuit.
3. Air-fry 4 donuts at a time at 350°F for 5 minutes. Air-fry 8 holes at a time for just 3 minutes.
4. Use a pastry brush to rub butter all over the donut and hole. Dip them into the sugar mixture.
5. Serve and enjoy!!!

French toast Soldiers

Preparation Time: 5 minutes
Cook Time: 10 minutes
Total Time: 15 minutes
Serves: 4

Ingredients:
- ¼ Cup Of Brown Sugar
- 1 Tbsp. Honey
- 1 Tsp Cinnamon
- Pinch Of Nutmeg
- 4 Slices Wholemeal Bread
- 2 Large Eggs
- ¼ Cup Of Whole Milk
- Pinch Of Icing
- Sugar

Cooking Instructions:
1. Cut each slice of your bread into 4 soldiers.
2. Put the rest of your ingredients except the icing sugar into a mixing bowl and combine well.
3. Soak each soldier into the mixture and then put it into the Air Fryer.
4. Put on 160ºC for 10 minutes. Turn them over so that both sides of the soldier can be well cooked.
5. Serve and enjoy!!!

Cinnamon Rolls

Preparation Time: 10 minutes
Cook Time: 9 minutes
Total Time: 19 minutes
Serves: 4

Ingredients:

- 1½ Tbsp. ground cinnamon
- Cream Cheese Glaze:
- 4 Oz cream cheese, softened
- 2 Tbsp. butter, softened
- 1 Lbs. frozen bread dough, thawed
- ¼ Cup of butter, melted and cooled
- ¾ Cup of brown sugar
- 1¼ Cups of powdered sugar
- ½ Tsp. vanilla

Cooking Instructions:

1. Roll the dough into 12-inch by 10-inch rectangle on a floured surface. Rub the dough with melted and leave some portion on dough uncovered.
2. Mix the cinnamon and brown sugar in a small bowl. Spread the mixture thoroughly over the buttered dough, leaving some portion uncovered.
3. Roll the dough into a log and push out any air pockets. Seal it together. Chop the log slowly with a sawing motion into 8 pieces.
4. Turn over the sides and cover with a kitchen towel. Keep the roll in the kitchen for 2 hours to rise. Put the butter and cream cheese in a bowl.
5. Microwave the mixture for 30 seconds at a time. Add the powdered sugar and stir. Put the vanilla extract and turn thoroughly. Keep aside.
6. Preheat the Air Fryer to 350°F. When the rolls have risen. Flip the rolls to the Air Fryer basket. Air-fry for 5 minutes. Flip the rolls over and air-fry for another 4 minutes.
7. Allow the rolls to cool before glazing. Sprinkle the cream cheese glaze on the cinnamon rolls.
8. Serve and enjoy!!!

AIR FRYER LUNCH RECIPES

Air Fryer Parmesan Shrimp

Preparation Time: 10 minutes
Cook Time: 10 minutes
Total Time: 20 minutes
Serves: 4

Ingredient:

- 1 Tsp. onion powder
- 2 Tbsp. olive oil
- Lemon, quartered
- 2 Lbs. jumbo cooked shrimp, peeled and deveined
- 4 Cloves garlic, minced
- 2/3 Cup of parmesan cheese, grated
- 1 Tsp. pepper
- ½ Tsp. oregano
- 1 Tsp. basil

Cooking Instructions:

1. Mix pepper, oregano, basil, onion powder, garlic, parmesan cheese and olive oil in a big bowl.
2. Dip shrimp into the mixture, place the shrimp in Air Fryer basket and spray with a non-sticky spray.
3. Cook at 350°F for 10 minutes.
4. Apply squeezed lemon on the shrimps.
5. Serve and enjoy!!!

Sriracha- Honey Chicken Wings

Preparation Time: 10 minutes
Cook Time: 33 minutes
Total Time: 43 minutes
Serves: 4

Ingredients:

- 1 ½ Tbsp. soy sauce
- 1 Tbsp. butter
- Juice of 1/2 lime
- Cilantro, chives, or scallions for garnish
- 1 Lbs. chicken wings
- ¼ Cup of honey
- 2 Tbsp. sriracha sauce

Cooking Instructions:

1. Preheat the Air Fryer to 360ºF.
2. Put the chicken wings in the Air Fryer basket, Air-fry for 30 minutes.
3. Flip to the other side of the chicken about every 7 minutes for proper cooking.
4. Put the sauce ingredients in a small sauce pan and boil for 3 minutes, while cooking the wings.
5. Once the wings are well cooked, coat it with the sauce, garnish with cilantro, chives or scallions.
6. Serve and enjoy!!!

Baked Potato

Preparation Time: 5 minutes
Cook Time: 35 minutes
Total Time: 40 minutes
Serves: 4

Ingredients:

- 1 Tbsp. Salt
- 2 Tbsp. Olive Oil
- 1 Tsp. Parsley
- 1 Tbsp. Garlic
- 3 Idaho or Russet Baking Potatoes

Cooking Instructions;

1. Rinse your potatoes and open air holes with a fork in the potatoes.
2. Sprinkle olive oil & seasonings on the potatoes.
3. Put them in the Air Fryer basket. Place them in the Air Fryer and cook.
4. Air-fry your potatoes at 392ºF for 35 minutes. Top with parsley.
5. Serve and enjoy!!!

Honey Chipotle Bacon Wrapped Tater Tot Bombs

Preparation Time: 5 minutes
Cook Time: 29 minutes
Total Time: 34 minutes
Serves: 8

Ingredients:

- ½ Tbsp. chipotle chili powder
- 16 Frozen Tater Tots
- 8 Slices of bacon
- 3 Tbsp. honey

Cooking Instructions:

1. Preheat your Air Fryer to 400ºF.
2. Chop the slices of bacon into half. Place the bacon slices on a plate.
3. Microwave the honey for about 15 seconds. Spread it on the bacon slices. Spread bacon with the chipotle powder.
4. Use the seasoned bacon to wrap each Tater Tot and place on the plate. Wrap loosely. Support the bottom with a toothpick.
5. Put the wrapped tots in the Air Fryer basket and cook for 14 minutes. Remove toothpicks.
6. Serve and enjoy!!!

Hot Dogs

Preparation Time: 3 minutes
Cook Time: 11 minutes
Total Time: 14 minutes
Serves: 2
Calories: 288 kcal

Ingredients:

- 2 Hot dogs
- 2 Tbsp. of grated cheese if desired
- 2 Hot dog buns

Cooking Instructions:

1. Preheat your Air Fryer to 390ºF for 4 minutes.
2. Put two hot dogs into the Air Fryer, Air-fry for 5 minutes.
3. Remove the hot dog from air fryer. Add cheese to the hot dog buns.
4. Put hot dog into the air fryer and cook for an additional 2 Minutes.
5. Serve and enjoy!!!

Chicken Nuggets

Preparation Time: 10 minutes
Cook Time: 8 minutes
Total Time: 18 minutes
Serves: 4
Calories: 364 kcal

Ingredients:

- 1 Boneless skinless chicken breast
- ¼ Tsp. salt
- 1/8 Tsp. black pepper
- ½ Cup of unsalted butter melted
- ½ Cup of breadcrumbs
- 2 Tbsp. grated Parmesan

Cooking Instructions:

1. Preheat Air Fryer to 390ºF for 4 minutes.
2. Cut any fat from chicken, chop into ½ inch thick slices. Spice the chicken pieces with pepper and salt.
3. Put melted butter in a bowl and breadcrumbs in another small bowl.
4. Coat each piece of chicken with butter and breadcrumbs too.
5. Put in the Air Fryer basket. Put in your Air Fryer and cook for 8 minutes.
6. Set unto a plate to cool when done.
7. Serve and enjoy!!!

Fried Green Tomatoes

Preparation Time: 5 minutes
Cook Time: 8 minutes
Total Time: 13 minutes
Serves: 4

Ingredients:

- 2 Green tomatoes
- Salt and pepper
- 1 Cup of Panko crumbs
- 1 Cup of yellow cornmeal
- olive oil
- ½ Cup of all-purpose flour
- 2 Large eggs
- ½ Cup of buttermilk

Cooking Instructions:

1. Chop tomatoes into ¼ inch slices. Dry with paper towels and season with pepper and salt.
2. Put flour in a small bowl. Mix together eggs and buttermilk in a bowl.
3. Mix cornmeal and Panko crumbs in a shallow dish. Preheat Air Fryer to 400°F.
4. Dredge the tomato slices in the flour, dip in egg mixture, and put panko crumb mixture into both end.
5. Spread some salt on them. Spray the Air Fryer basket with oil and put 4 tomato slices in basket.
6. Spray the tops with oil. Air-fry for 5 minutes. Transfer tomatoes, spray with oil and air-fry 3 more minutes.
7. Serve and enjoy!!!

Chicken Parmesan

Preparation Time: 10 minutes
Cook Time: 20 minutes
Total Time: 30 minutes
Serves: 4
Calories: 251 kcal

Ingredients:

- 6 Tbsp. seasoned breadcrumbs
- 2 Tbsp. grated Parmesan cheese
- 1 Tbsp. butter, melted
- 2 Chicken breast
- 6 Tbsp. reduced fat mozzarella cheese
- ½ Cup of marinara
- Cooking spray

Cooking Instructions:

1. Preheat the Air Fryer to 360°F for 9 minutes. Spray the basket with the cooking spray.
2. In a small bowl, mix parmesan cheese and breadcrumbs. Put the butter in another bowl and melt it.
3. Spread the butter on the chicken and dip into parmesan cheese mixture.
4. Put 2 pieces in the Air Fryer basket and mist the top with oil.
5. Air-fry for 6 minutes turn and top each with sauce and shredded mozzarella cheese. Air-fry for 3 more minutes.
6. Repeat with the remaining 2 pieces.
7. Serve and enjoy!!!

Garlic Parmesan Chicken Wings

Preparation Time: 10 minutes
Cook Time: 28 minutes
Total Time: 38 minutes
Serves: 4

Ingredients:

- 2 Tsp. minced garlic
- 2 Tsp. fresh parsley, chopped
- 1 Tsp salt
- 2 Lbs. wings and drumettes
- ¾ Cup of grated parmesan cheese
- 1 Tsp pepper

Cooking Instructions:

1. Preheat the Air Fryer to 400ºF for 4 minutes.
2. Dry chicken pieces with a paper towel.
3. Combine parsley, pepper, parmesan cheese, garlic, and salt together in a bowl.
4. Put chicken pieces in cheese mixture until it is well dredge.
5. Put chicken in bottom of the Air Fryer basket for 12 minutes.
6. Use fork to transfer chicken, after 12 minutes. Air-fry again for 12 minutes.
7. Pick chicken from basket with tongs and spread with parmesan cheese and parsley.
8. Serve and enjoy!!!

Crispy Breaded Pork Chops

Preparation Time: 10 minutes
Cook Time: 24 minutes
Total Time: 34 minutes
Serves: 6
Calories: 378 kcal

Ingredients:
- $1/3$ Cup of crushed cornflakes crumbs
- 2 Tbsp. grated parmesan cheese
- 1¼ Tsp. sweet paprika
- Kosher salt
- 1 Large egg, beaten
- ½ Cup of panko crumbs
- ¼ Tsp. chili powder
- $1/8$ Tsp. black pepper
- ½ Tsp. garlic powder
- ½ Tsp. onion powder olive oil spray
- 6 Centre cut boneless pork chops, fat trimmed

Cooking Instruction:
1. Preheat the air fryer to 400ºF for 12 minutes and oil the basket.
2. Cut the pork and Season it on both sides with kosher salt.
3. Mix kosher salt, paprika, garlic powder, onion powder, chili powder, panko, cornflake crumbs, parmesan cheese and black pepper in a large bowl.
4. Put the beaten egg in bowl. Put the pork into the egg, and latter crumb mixture.
5. Place 3 of the cut pork into the prepared Air Fryer basket and sprinkle the top with oil, When the Air Fryer is ready.
6. Air-fry for about 12 minutes and sprinkle both sides with oil. Keep aside and follow the same process for the remaining pork. Serve and enjoy!!!

Beef Empanadas

Preparation Time: 10 minutes
Cook Time: 16 minutes
Total Time: 26 minutes
Serves: 4
Calories: 178 kcal
Ingredients:
- 1 Egg white, whisked
- 8 Goya empanada discs thawed
- 1 Cup picadillo
- 1 Tsp. water

Cooking Instructions:
1. Preheat the Air Fryer to 325ºF for 8 minutes. Spray the Air Fryer basket with cooking spray.
2. Put 2 Tbsp. of picadillo in the center of Goya empanada disc. Fold into two and use a fork to close the edges and do same to other dough.
3. Mix the egg whites with water then brush the tops of the empanadas.
4. Air-fry 3 at a time for 8 minutes. Repeat same with other empanadas.
5. Serve and enjoy!!!

Sweet Potato Tots

Preparation Time: 10 minutes
Cook Time: 14 minutes
Total Time: 24 minutes
Serves: 25

Ingredients:
- ½ Tsp. coriander
- 2 Cups of sweet potato puree
- ½ Tsp. salt
- ½ Tsp. cumin
- ½ Cup of Panko breadcrumbs
- Spray oil

Cooking Instructions:
1. Preheat the Air Fryer to 200°C. Combine all ingredients together in a large mixing bowl.
2. Make some tots of 1 tbsp. and put them into plates.
3. Coat with spray oil. Turn the tots around to spray the bottoms with oil.
4. Arrange tots on the Air Fryer basket with care, so there is gap between them. Cook in 3 batches.
5. Air-fry for 7 minutes. Turn them over and keep them for some minutes.
6. Air-fry for 7 more minutes.
7. Serve and enjoy!!!

Baked Thai Peanut Chicken Egg Rolls

Preparation Time: 10 minutes
Cook Time: 8 minutes
Total Time: 18 minutes
Serves: 4

Ingredients:

- 4 Egg roll wrappers
- 2 Cup of rotisserie chicken shredded
- ¼ Cup of Thai peanut sauce
- Non-stick cooking spray
- 1 Medium carrot very thinly sliced
- 3 Green onions chopped
- ¼ Red bell pepper julienned

Cooking Instructions:

1. Preheat Air Fryer to 390°F. Throw the chicken with the Thai peanut sauce, in a small mixing bowl.
2. On a clean dry surface, spread the egg roll wrappers. Arrange ¼ carrot, onions and bell pepper on the third bottom of the egg roll wrapper.
3. Spread ½ cup of the chicken mixture on top of the vegetables. Wet the edges of the wrapper with water. Roll wrapper from side to centre.
4. Do the same to the remaining wrappers. Spray both sides of the egg rolls with non-stick cooking spray.
5. Put the egg rolls in the Air Fryer and Air-fry at 390°F for 8 minutes. Cut into two and top with additional Thai Peanut Sauce.
6. Serve and enjoy!!!

Crispy Roasted Onion Potatoes

Preparation Time: 3 minutes
Cook Time: 20 minutes
Total Time: 23 minutes
Serves: 4

Ingredients:

- 2 Tbsp. olive oil
- 1 Envelope Lipton onion soup mix
- 2 Lbs. baby red potatoes

Cooking Instructions:

1. Chop the potatoes and throw them in the olive oil in a bowl.
2. Put the onion soup mix and stir.
3. Put the potatoes in the Air Fryer basket and Air-fry at 390°F for 20 minutes.
4. Serve and enjoy!!!

Sweet Potato Fries

Preparation Time: 3 minutes
Cook Time: 20 minutes
Total Time: 10 minutes
Serves: 2
Calories: 221 kcal

Ingredients:
- ½ Tsp. garlic powder
- ¼ Tsp. sweet paprika
- ½ Tsp. kosher salt
- Fresh black pepper, to taste
- 2 Medium peeled sweet potatoes
- 2 Tsp. olive oil

Cooking Instruction:
1. Preheat Air Fryer to 400°F for 8 minutes.
2. Spray the Air Fryer basket with oil.
3. Chop each potato into ¼ inch thick fries.
4. Toss with garlic powder, black pepper, oil, paprika and salt.
5. Air-fry in 3 batches for about 8 minutes. Flip over half way.
6. Serve and enjoy!!!

AIR FRYER FISH & SEAFOOD RECIPES

Air-Grilled Honey-Glazed Salmon

Preparation Time: 10 minutes
Cook Time: 14 minutes
Total Time: 21 minutes
Serves: 4
Ingredients:
- 6 tbsp. Honey
- 6 Tsp. Soy Sauce
- 2 Pieces. Salmon Fillets
- 3 Tsp. Hon Mirin
- 1 Tsp. Water

Cooking instructions:
1. Combine together soy sauce, honey, Hon Mirin and water.
2. Put some of the mixture in a different bowl, keep aside.
3. Mix together the marinade and the salmon mixture, keep aside to marinate for at least 2 hours.
4. Preheat the Air Fryer at 180°C. Air-fry the salmon for 8 minutes, turn over halfway, air-fry for another 5 minutes.
5. Apply some marinade mixture on the salmon every 3 minutes.
6. To make the sauce, put the remaining sauce in a pan and cook for 1 minute. Top with salmon.
7. Serve and enjoy!!!

Cajun Shrimp

Preparation Time: 10 minutes
Cook Time: 5 minutes
Total Time: 15 minutes
Serves: 2

Ingredients:

- ¼ Tsp. smoked paprika
- 1 Pinch of salt
- 1 Tbsp. olive oil
- ½ Lbs. tiger shrimp
- ¼ Tsp. cayenne pepper
- ½ Tsp. old bay seasoning

Cooking Instructions:

1. Preheat the air fryer to 390°F.
2. Mix together all the ingredients, in a bowl.
3. Dredge the shrimp with the oil and the spices.
4. Put the shrimp into the Air Fryer basket and Air-fry for 5 minutes.
5. Serve and enjoy!!!

Fried Shrimp

Preparation Time: 10 minutes
Cook Time: 15 minutes
Total Time: 25 minutes
Serves: 4

Ingredients:
- Yellow Mustard
- Tony's Chachere
- Raw Shrimp, peeled
- Fish Fry
- Cooking Spray

Cooking Instructions:
1. Prepare your shrimp and put in a plate. Spread with Tony's Chachere. Sprinkle the shrimp with mustard and combine all together.
2. Put fish fry in a small zip bag and add a few shrimp to the fish fry. Zip the bag and shake to dredge the shrimp. Do same with rest of the shrimps.
3. Put the shrimp without over lapping in the Air Fryer basket. Spray with cooking spray to coat the fish fry.
4. Put Air Fryer basket into the Air Fryer and Air-fry at 330°F for 8 minutes.
5. Turn over your shrimp, spray again and Air-fry at 330°F for 7 minutes.
6. Serve and enjoy!!!

Jalapeno Artichoke and Crab Dip

Preparation Time: 10 minutes
Cook Time: 5 minutes
Total Time: 15 minutes
Serves: 4

Ingredients:

- Fresh parsley to taste
- Fresh ground black pepper
- 1 Container of ready jalapeno and artichoke dip
- 1 Lbs. crabmeat

Cooking Instructions:

1. Put the jalapeno and artichoke dip with crabmeat in a bowl. Combine lightly.
2. Put black pepper and parsley to taste and stir.
3. Top with crackers, toasts or vegetables.
4. Serve and enjoy!!!

Tuna Poke, Raw Fish Salad

Preparation Time: 10 minutes
Cook Time: 5 minutes
Total Time: 15 minutes
Serves: 2

Ingredients:
- ½ Lb. ahi tuna, sashimi grade
- ½ Tsp. sriracha
- 1 Tsp. roasted sesame seed
- 1 Tbsp. soy sauce
- 1 Green onion, finely chopped
- ½ Tsp. sesame oil

Cooking Instructions:
1. In a small mixing bowl, Chop the ahi tuna into ½ inch and put green onion.
2. Mix together the sriracha, soy sauce and sesame oil in a bowl.
3. Turn the sauce in the tuna and thoroughly mix them. Spray with roasted sesame seeds.
4. Serve and enjoy!!!

Creamy Shrimp Homemade Spinach Pasta

Preparation Time: 10 minutes
Cook Time: 4 minutes
Total Time: 14 minutes
Serves: 3

Ingredients:

- 8 Oz. shrimp
- Salt and pepper
- ¼ Cup of grated parmesan
- 1 Small onion, finely chopped
- 3 Garlic cloves, finely chopped
- 1 Tbsp. olive oil
- 3 Oz. cream cheese
- ½ Cup of milk
- 1 Tbsp. butter

Cooking Instructions

1. Heat 1 tbsp. butte sauté onion and garlic in a medium sauce pan for about a minute.
2. Reduce the heat, put milk and cream cheese stirring continuously to thicken the mixture. Put salt, heavy cream, and pepper to taste.
3. Put the butter in a fry pan fry the shrimps. Make sure both sides are fried properly.
4. Put the Parmesan into the cream sauce and remove from heat. Stir and put the shrimp. Sprinkle the sauce on the spinach pasta.
5. Serve and enjoy!!!

Chunky Crab Cakes

Preparation Time: 10 minutes
Cook Time: 10 minutes
Total Time: 20 minutes
Serves: 4

Ingredients:

- 1 Tsp. Dijon mustard
- ½ Cup of panko
- Vegetable oil
- 1 Tsp. Worcestershire sauce
- 1 Tsp. Old Bay seasoning
- Fresh pepper
- 1 Large egg
- 2 Tbsp. mayonnaise
- ¼ Cup of finely chopped fresh parsley
- 1 Lb. lump crab meat

Cooking Instructions

1. Mix together Dijon mustard, egg, Old Bay, mayonnaise and Worcestershire in a small bowl.
2. Put the chopped parsley into the mixture and turn them into the crab meat. Put the panko to the mixture, mix properly, and cover.
3. Add them in refrigerator for about an hour. Make them into 7 crab cakes of 1 inch thickness.
4. On a medium heat, preheat a large non-stick pan with vegetable oil. Air-fry both sides of the crab cakes. Flip onto a serving plate.
5. Serve and enjoy!!!

Oden Japanese Dish

Preparation Time: 10 minutes
Cook Time: 1 hour 7 minutes
Total Time: 17 minutes
Serves: 3

Ingredients:
- Dried bonito fish
- 15 inches Kombu
- 50 Ml of sake
- ⅓ Cup of soy sauce
- Dashi soup for the oden
- 2 Litters of water
- 1½ Tbsp. sugar
- Tied konnyaku
- Plate of various fish paste stick and patties
- Oden ingredients of your choice
- 2 Daikon radish, peeled and shred into 1 ½ inch

Cooking Instructions:
1. Rinse the Kombu, chop into small strip and tie a knot.
2. Put the dried bonito and Kombu into hot water extract the flavour. Use a clean cloth to strain the dashi soup.
3. Mix the daikon radish in the dashi soup and Air-fry for about minutes. Prepare the konnyaku by making a slit in the middle and put on end through the slit.
4. Boil water in a large pot, put all the ingredients and cook for an hour.
5. Serve and enjoy!!!

Crumbed Fish

Preparation Time: 10 minutes
Cook Time: 12 minutes
Total Time: 22 minutes
Serves: 2

Ingredients:

- 1 Egg, whisked
- 4 Tbsp. vegetable oil
- 100g Breadcrumbs
- 1 Lemon
- 4 Fish fillets

Cooking Instructions:

1. Preheat your Air Fryer to 180ºC.
2. Combine together the breadcrumbs and oil. Stir.
3. Bury the fish fillets into the egg then shake thoroughly.
4. Bury the fish fillets again into the breadcrumb mixture.
5. Put them in the Air Fryer and air-fry for 12 minutes. Top with Lemon.
6. Serve and enjoy!!!

Zesty Crumbed Fish Fillets

Preparation: 15 minutes
Cook Time: 10 minutes
Total Time: 25 minutes
Serves: 4

Ingredients:

- ¾ Cup of bread crumbs
- 500g Tilapia fillets
- 2 Tsp. butter
- 1 Packet dry ranch-style dressing mix
- 2 ½ Tbsp. vegetable oil

Cooking Instructions:

1. Put the bread crumbs in a bowl.
2. Combine the dressing mix and oil to make a paste, in a shallow dish. Dip the tilapia fillets with the paste then dredge in the bread crumbs.
3. In a frying pan, heat the butter over a medium of heat to melt.
4. Put the fillets in the frying pan and Air-fry for 5 minutes on both side.
5. Serve and enjoy!!!

Marinated Spicy Fish Fillets

Preparation Time: 20 minutes
Cook Time: 40 minutes
Total Time: 1 hour
Serves: 8

Ingredients:

- 1 Tbsp. salt
- 1 Tbsp. ground black pepper
- 1 Litre oil for frying
- 2 Cups of instant mashed potato
- ½ Cup of plain flour
- 2 Tbsp. seasoning salt
- ½ Cup of teriyaki sauce
- 1 Cup of stir fry sauce
- 8 Fillets white fish, such as hake
- 1 Tbsp. chilli powder
- 1 Tbsp. garlic powder

Cooking Instructions:

1. Combine the teriyaki sauce and stir fry sauce in a bowl. Put the fish fillets in the mixture and marinated for about 15 minutes.
2. Preheat the oil in an Air Fryer at 185°C. Combine together the instant mashed potato, flour, garlic powder, salt, pepper, seasoning salt, and chilli powder in a small bowl.
3. Put each marinated fish fillet into the mixture to dredge. Air-fry the fish in the heated oil, 2 fillets at a time for about 5 minutes.
4. Serve and enjoy!!!

Fried Catfish

Preparation Time: 5 minutes
Cook Time: 1 hour
Total Time: 1 hour 5 minutes
Serves: 4
Calories: 208 kcal

Ingredients:

- ¼ Cup of seasoned fish fry
- 1 Tbsp. olive oil
- 4 Catfish fillets
- 1 Tbsp. chopped parsley

Cooking Instructions:

1. Preheat Air Fryer to 400°C. Wash the catfish and dry.
2. Put the fish fry seasoning in a Ziploc bag. Place the catfish to the bag, one at a time.
3. Close the bag and shake, making sure that the whole fillets is dredge with seasoning. Sprinkle olive oil on the top of each filet.
4. Put the fillet in the Air Fryer basket. Close and Air-fry for about 10 minutes. Turn the fish.
5. Air-fry for another 10 minutes. Turn the fish again and air-fry for about 3 minutes more. Top with parsley.
6. Serve and enjoy!!!

Crispy Oat Crumbed Fish

Preparation Time: 5 minutes
Cook Time: 15 minutes
Total Time: 20 minutes
Serves: 4

Ingredients:

- Vegetable oil for frying
- 2 Tbsp. plain flour for coating
- 2 Cups (150g) of instant rolled oats
- 1 Egg, whisked
- 1/3 Cup (75ml) of milk
- 4 Fish fillets
- Salt and freshly ground black pepper, to taste

Cooking Instructions:

1. In a small mixing flat plate, put the flour and the oats. In a small mixing bowl, Whisk together the egg and milk.
2. Dip the fish fillet into flour and coat properly. Bury in egg mixture and allow the excess to drip off then coat the fillet with oats.
3. Repeat with the other fillets. Using a medium high heat, warm your oil in a frying pan.
4. Add fish into the oil and Air-fry for 2 ½. Flip over to the other sides and Air-fry for another 2 ½ minutes. Add salt and pepper to taste.
5. Serve and enjoy!!!

Coconut Shrimp with Spicy Marmalade Sauce

Preparation Time: 10 minutes
Cook Time: 20 minutes
Total Time: 30 minutes
Serves: 2
Calories: 623 kcal

Ingredients:

- ½ Tsp. cayenne pepper
- ¼ Tsp. kosher salt
- ¼ Tsp. fresh ground pepper
- ½ Cup of orange marmalade
- 1 Tbsp. Honey
- 8 Large shrimp shelled and deveined
- 8 Oz coconut milk
- ½ Cup of shredded sweetened coconut
- ½ Cup of panko bread
- 1 Tsp. mustard
- ¼ Tsp. hot sauce

Cooking Instructions:

1. Wash the shrimp and keep aside.
2. Mix coconut milk and season with pepper and salt in a bowl and keep aside, combine together the coconut, panko, cayenne pepper, salt and pepper in a another bowl.
3. Coat the shrimp in the coconut milk, then the panko mixture one at a time, put them in the Air Fryer basket.
4. Do same to all the shrimps. Air-fry the shrimp for 20 minutes at 350ºF.
5. Mix together the mustard, marmalade, honey, and hot sauce. While the shrimp are cooking. Top with the sauce.
6. Serve and enjoy!!!

Beer Battered Fish Fillets

Preparation Time: 10 minutes
Cook Time: 20 minutes
Total Time: 45 minutes
Serves: 8

Ingredients:
- ½ Tsp. dried dill
- ¾ Cup of beer
- ½ Cup of milk
- 2 Eggs
- 1 Cup of plain flour
- 1 Tsp. salt
- 1 Tsp. baking powder
- 1kg White fish fillets
- 2 Litres of vegetable oil, for frying

Cooking Instructions:
1. Combine together baking powder, flour, salt, and dill in a big bowl, add beer, milk and eggs and mix thoroughly.
2. Put fish fillets in batter mixture and dip well for 15 minutes to coat.
3. Preheat the Air Fryer to 180°C.
4. Put fish in hot oil and Air-fry for 5 minutes. Air-fry fish in batches.
5. Serve and enjoy!!!

AIR FRYER POULTRY RECIPES

KFC Chicken Strips

Preparation Time: 10 minutes
Cook Time: 12 minutes
Total Time: 22 minutes
Serves: 8
Calories: 94 kcal

Ingredients:

- 15ml Plain Oats
- 5 ml KFC Spice Blend get our recipe here
- 75ml Bread Crumbs
- 1 Chicken Breast chopped into strips
- 15ml Desiccated Coconut
- 50g Plain Flour
- 1 Small Egg beaten
- Salt & Pepper

Cooking Instructions:

1. Cut chicken breast into strips.
2. Put coconut, salt, oats, KFC spice blend, bread crumbs and pepper in a bowl and mix.
3. Put egg in a separate bowl and put plain flour in another bowl.
4. Coat chicken breast strips in the plain flour, put in the egg and finally in the spicy layer.
5. Put in the Air Fryer and Air-fry at 180°C for 8 minutes.
6. Flip over and then cook for another 4 minutes on 160°C.
7. Serve and enjoy!!!

Chicken Nugget

Preparation Time: 15 minutes
Cook Time: 8 minutes
Total Time: 23 minutes
Serves: 6

Ingredients:

- 1 Cup of dill pickle juice
- 3 Tbsp. powdered sugar
- 2 Tsp salt
- 1½ Tsp. pepper
- ½ Tsp. paprika
- Olive oil spritz
- 1 Lbs. boneless skinless chicken breasts, cut into pieces about 1 inch in size
- 1 Egg
- 1 Cup of milk
- 1½ Cups of flour

Cooking Instructions:

1. Mix chicken chunks and pickle juice and marinate in the freezer for about 30 minutes. Mix milk and egg together.
2. Keep aside. Mix together all the dry ingredients and stir. Set aside. Preheat Air Fryer to 370°F.
3. Take the chicken from freezer, drain and put each into the dry mixture, liquid mixture and back to the dry mixture to coat, shake off excess.
4. Air-fry in a single layer of chicken for 8 minutes. Turnover and spritz with olive oil halfway.
5. Serve and enjoy!!!

Buttermilk Chicken

Preparation Time: 6 hours
Cook Time: 8 minutes
Total Time: 6 hours 8 minutes
Serves: 6

Ingredients:

- 800g Store-bought chicken thighs
- 1 Tbsp. baking powder
- 1 Tbsp. garlic powder
- 1 Tbsp. paprika powder
- 1 Tsp. salt
- 2 Cups of buttermilk
- 2 Tsp. salt
- 2 Tsp. black pepper
- 1 Tsp. cayenne pepper
- 2 Cups of all-purpose flour

Cooking Instructions:

1. Wash chicken thighs to remove excess fat and dirt, and dry with paper towels.
2. Mix together chicken pieces, paprika, black pepper and salt in a big bowl to dredge. Add buttermilk over until chicken is dredge.
3. Put in the refrigerator for at least 6 hours. Preheat the Air Fryer at 180°C.
4. Mix flour, baking powder, paprika, pepper and salt in separate bowl. Take the chicken one at a time from the buttermilk and coat in seasoned flour.
5. Shake off all excess flour and flip to a plate. Put them on the fryer basket, skin side up, and into the Air Fryer.
6. Air-fry for 8 minutes. Flip chicken pieces over to a tray and Air-fry for another 10 minutes. Leave to drain on paper towel.
7. Serve and enjoy!!!

Leftover Turkey & Cheese Calzone

Preparation Time: 10 minutes
Cook Time: 10 minutes
Total Time: 20 minutes
Serves: 4
Calories: 158 kcal

Ingredients:

- 4 Tbsp. Homemade Tomato Sauce
- 1 Tbsp. Tomato Puree
- 1 Tsp. Oregano
- 1 Tsp. Basil
- 1 Tsp. Thyme
- Salt & Pepper
- Leftover Turkey brown meat shredded
- 100 g Cheddar Cheese
- 25 g Mozzarella Cheese grated
- 25 g Back Bacon diced
- 1 Large Egg beaten

Cooking Instructions:

1. Preheat the Air Fryer to 180ºc.
2. Roll out your pizza dough to small pizzas. Mix together all the seasonings as well as the tomato sauce and puree in a small mixing bowl.
3. Add a layer of tomato sauce to your pizza without touching edge with a 1cm space using a cooking brush.
4. Top your pizza with your turkey, bacon and cheese to one side. Using cooking brush again, spread beaten egg in the 1cm gap around your pizza edge.
5. Wrap your pizza edge over to resemble an uncooked Cornish pasty and brushed with more egg. Air-fry at 180ºC for 10 minutes.
6. Serve and enjoy!!!

Chicken Breast

Preparation Time: 15 minutes
Cook Time: 10 minutes
Total Time: 20 minutes
Serves: 4
Calories: 188 kcal

Ingredients:

- 1 Lbs. boneless skinless chicken breasts
- 1 Tbsp. olive oil

Breading:

- ½ Tsp. paprika
- 1/8 Tsp. garlic powder
- ¼ Cup of bread crumbs
- ½ Tsp. salt
- ¼ Tsp. black pepper
- 1/8 Tsp. onion powder
- 1/16 Tsp. cayenne pepper

Cooking Instructions:

1. Preheat the Air Fryer to 390°F.
2. Cut chicken breasts in half to make two thinned chicken breast.
3. Spread each side with small quantity of olive oil.
4. Mix the breading ingredients together and coat the chicken breasts in the breading to dredge. Shake off excess.
5. Put in the Air Fryer. Air-fry for 4 minutes, turn and Air-fry for two more minutes. Cut one into half to see if they are done.
6. Serve and enjoy!!!

Lemon Pepper Chicken

Preparation Time: 3 minutes
Cook Time: 15 minutes
Total Time: 18 minutes
Servings: 1
Calories: 140 kcal

Ingredients:

- 1 Chicken Breast
- 2 Lemons rind and juice
- 1 Tbsp. Chicken Seasoning
- 1 Tsp. Garlic Puree
- Handful Black Peppercorns
- Salt & Pepper

Cooking Instructions:

1. Preheat the Air Fryer to 180°C.
2. Place a large sheet of foil and put all the seasonings and the lemon rind.
3. Spread out your chicken breasts on a chopping board and cut off any excess fat or bones.
4. Season both sides with pepper and salt. Apply the chicken seasoning into both sides again. Put it in the foil sheet and apply it to be well season.
5. Close it very tight to help get the flavour into it. Slap it with a rolling pin to flatten it out and release more flavour.
6. Put it in the Air Fryer for 15 minutes and check inside to know if it is done.
7. Serve and enjoy!!!

Turkey Breast with Maple Mustard Glaze

Preparation Time: 10 minutes
Cook Time: 59 minutes
Total Time: 1 hour 9 minutes
Serves 4

Ingredients:

- 2 Tbsp. Dijon mustard
- 1 Tbsp. butter
- 1 Tsp. dried thyme
- ½ Tsp. dried sage
- ½ Tsp. smoked paprika
- 1 Tsp. Salt
- 2 Tsp. olive oil
- 5 Lbs. whole turkey breast
- ½ Tsp. freshly ground black pepper
- ¼ Cup of maple syrup

Cooking Instructions:

1. Preheat Air Fryer to 350ºF. Spread the olive oil on the turkey breast.
2. Mix the paprika, thyme, sage, pepper and salt and apply spice mixture to the outside of the turkey breast.
3. Flip the seasoned turkey breast to the Air Fryer basket. Air-fry at 350ºF for 25 minutes.
4. Flip the turkey breast on its side and Air-fry for another 12 minutes. Turn it on the opposite side and Air-fry for another 12 minutes.
5. Mix the maple syrup, mustard and butter in a saucepan. Flip over the turkey breast and spread the glaze all over the turkey.
6. Air-fry for another 5 minutes. Remove the turkey and allow it to cool for sometimes, cover lightly with foil, for at least 5 minutes before chopping.
7. Serve and enjoy!!!

Thanksgiving Turkey

Preparation Time: 15 minutes
Cook Time: 35 minutes
Total Time: 50 minutes
Serves: 3

Ingredients:

- 1 Tsp. ground rosemary
- 1 Tsp. kosher salt
- 1 Tsp. dried thyme
- 1 (2 Lbs.) Bone-in, skin-on turkey breast
- Olive oil, for brushing
- ½ Tsp. freshly ground black pepper
- ½ Tsp. dried sage
- ½ Tsp. garlic powder
- ½ Tsp. paprika
- ½ Tsp. dark brown sugar

Cooking Instructions:

1. Using a small mixing bowl, mix together the rosemary, brown sugar, pepper, sage, salt, garlic powder, paprika and thyme.
2. Rub olive oil on both sides of the turkey breast with the above mixture. Place the turkey skin-side down in the Air Fryer basket.
3. Air-fry at 360° F for about 20 minutes. While the cooking time completes, flip over to the other side and air-fry at 165°F for more 15 minutes.
4. Allow it to cool for about 10 minutes.
5. Serve and enjoy!!!

Honey Garlic Wings

Preparation Time: 10 minutes
Cook Time: 24 minutes
Total Time: 34 minutes
Serves: 4

Ingredients:

- ½ Cup of honey
- 3 Tbsp. corn starch (optional)
- ½ Cup of brown sugar
- 2 Tsp. of minced garlic
- ½ Lbs of chicken wings
- ½ Cup of soy sauce
- 2 Tsp. of ground ginger

Cooking Instructions:

1. Keep the chicken wings in the Air Fryer. Air-fry at 400ºF for 12 minutes.
2. When cooking time completes, flip the chicken over to the other side and air-fry for another 12 minutes.
3. In a saucepan, prepare the sauce and put your garlic, ginger, soy sauce, honey, brown sugar and give everything s good stir.
4. If you are not satisfied with the thickness, add corn starch, stir properly and remove from heat.
5. Coat both sides of the chicken with the sauce.
6. Serve and enjoy!!!

Spatchcock Chicken

Preparation Time: 1 minute
Cook Time: 50 minutes
Total Time: 51 minutes
Serves: 4
Calories: 400 kcal

Ingredients:

- 1 Tbsp. Garlic Puree
- Salt and Pepper
- 2 Tsp. Olive Oil
- 1 Tsp. Mixed Herbs
- 0.9 Kilo. Spatchcock Chicken

Cooking Instructions:

1. Gather all the seasonings and mix together.
2. Put garlic puree and olive oil. Stir thoroughly.
3. Keep your chicken on the air fryer grilling pan.
4. Rub the seasoning mixture and coat properly.
5. Air-fry at 360°F for 25 minutes on each side. Top with rice and salad.
6. Serve and enjoy!!!

Lemon Dijon Chicken Wings

Preparation Time: 10 minutes
Cook Time: 26 minutes
Total Time: 36 minutes
Serves: 4

Ingredients:

- 2 Tsp. minced garlic
- 2 Lbs. chicken wings
- 4 Tbsp. olive oil
- 1 Tsp. salt
- 1 Tsp. pepper
- 1 Tbsp. lemon juice
- 2 Tbsp. Dijon mustard

Cooking Instructions:

1. Preheat the Air Fryer to 400°F. Mix together the lemon juice, Dijon mustard, olive oil, garlic, salt, and pepper in a small mixing bowl.
2. Toss in the chicken wings. Keep half of the chicken into the Air Fryer. Air-fry for 13 minutes.
3. Flip them over and air-fry for another 13 minutes. Repeat this for all the chickens. Flip them onto a serving plate.
4. Serve and enjoy!!!

Whole Roasted Lemon & Rosemary Chicken

Preparation Time: 10 minutes
Cook Time: 50 minutes
Total Time: 1 hour
Serves: 2

Ingredients:

- 4 Lbs. whole chicken
- Juice of 2 lemons
- 2 Sprigs of rosemary

Cooking Instructions:

1. Rinse the chicken. Dip them into the lemon juice and spray the rosemary.
2. Sprinkle olive oil over the chicken and air-fry at 330°F for 30 minutes.
3. Turn the chicken to the other side and air fry for another 20 minutes.
4. Serve and enjoy!!!

Shredded Chicken

Preparation Time: 2 minutes
Cook Time: 15 minutes
Total Time: 17 minutes
Serves: 2
Calories: 583 kcal

Ingredients:

- 1 Tsp. Honey
- 1 Tsp. Mustard
- 2 Large Chicken Breasts
- Salt and Pepper
- 1 Tsp. Garlic Puree

Cooking Instructions:

1. Gather all the marinade ingredients into the air fryer baking pan. Stir.
2. Keep the chicken into the mixture and put pepper and salt for seasoning. Air-fry at 360°F for 15 minutes.
3. After about 7 minutes cut the chicken into 3 to enable it cook properly. Remove the chicken when it is done.
4. Allow it to cool for about 2 minutes. Cut the chicken into small sizes.
5. Serve and enjoy!!!

Chinese Chicken Wings

Preparation Time: 10 minutes
Cook Time: 25 minutes
Total Time: 35 minutes
Serves: 3
Ingredients:
- 2 Lbs. of chicken wings
- 1 Cup of soy sauce
- 1 Tbsp. of garlic powder
- 1 Cup of brown sugar

Cooking Instructions:
1. Pour garlic powder, soy sauce and brown sugar into a small saucepan. Stir and boil them.
2. Bury the chicken into the sauce and refrigerate for about 30 minutes.
3. Preheat your Air Fryer to 360ºF. Air-fryer for 15 minutes.
4. Turn them over to the other side and Air-fry for another 10 minutes.
5. Serve and enjoy!!!

Honey BBQ Chicken Wings

Preparation Time: 10 minutes
Cook Time: 24 minutes
Total Time: 34 minutes
Serves: 4

Ingredients:

- 12 Chicken wings
- ½ Cup of flour
- ½ Cup of barbecue sauce
- 1 Tsp. of salt
- ½ Cup of honey
- 1 Tsp. of pepper

Cooking Instructions:

1. Preheat the Air Fryer to 350°F.
2. In a small mixing bowl, put the chicken wings, flour, salt, and pepper. Coat the chicken wings properly.
3. Place wings into the Air Fryer and Air-fry for 12 minutes. Turn them over to the other side and Air-fry for another 12 minutes.
4. In a small mixing bowl, put the honey and BBQ sauce and mix properly. Dip the chicken wings when they are done into the honey and BBQ sauce and coat properly.
5. Serve and enjoy!!!

KFC Popcorn Chicken

Preparation Time: 10 minutes
Cook Time: 12 minutes
Total Time: 22 minutes
Serves: 12
Calories: 44 kcal

Ingredients:

- 1 Chicken Breast
- 1 Small Egg beaten
- 50g Plain Flour
- 2ml KFC Spice Blend
- Salt and Pepper
- 60ml Bread Crumbs

Cooking Instructions:

1. Mince your chicken in a food blender. In a small bowl, put the flour while you put the beaten egg a separate bowl.
2. In another mixing bowl, put KFC spice blend, bread crumbs, salt and pepper and mix properly.
3. Prepare your chicken like balls shape, roll in the flour, egg and the spiced bread crumbs one after the other.
4. Air-fry the chicken at 180ºC for about 12 minutes.
5. Serve and enjoy!!!

Chicken Wrapped In Bacon

Preparation Time: 3 minutes
Cook Time: 15 minutes
Total Time: 18 minutes
Serves: 6
Calories: 109 kcal

Ingredients:

- 1 Chicken Breast
- 6 Back Bacon
- 1 Tbsp. Garlic Soft Cheese

Cooking Instructions:

1. Shred the chicken breast into 6 small pieces.
2. Place the bacon rashers with small garlic soft cheese.
3. Roll the chicken on top of the cheese. Cover them using a cocktail stick.
4. Air-fry at 180°C for 15 minutes.
5. Serve and enjoy!!!

Tangy Barbecue Chicken

Preparation Time: 10 minutes
Cook Time: 15 minutes
Total Time: 25 minutes
Serves: 4

Ingredients:

- 4 Boneless Skinless Chicken Breast
- 5 Tbsp. of balsamic vinegar
- ¼ Cup of brown sugar
- 3 Tbsp. of Dijon mustard
- 3 Tbsp. of soy sauce
- 3 Tbsp. of olive oil

Cooking Instructions:

1. In a bowl, Mix together all the ingredients.
2. Put chicken and put in the refrigerator for 30 minutes.
3. Keep the chicken into the Air Fryer basket and air-fry at 380°F for 15 minutes.
4. Serve and enjoy!!!

AIR FRYER BEEF & PORK RECIPES

Pork Taquitos

Preparation Time: 10 minutes
Cook Time: 10 minutes
Total Time: 20 minutes
Serves: 2
Calories: 256 kcal

Ingredients:

- 1 Lime, juiced
- 3 Cups of cooked shredded pork tenderloin or chicken
- 2 ½ Cups of fat free shredded mozzarella
- 10 Small flour tortillas
- Cooking spray

Cooking Instructions:

1. Preheat Air Fryer to 380°F.
2. Spread lime juice over pork and combine together.
3. Microwave the tortillas, 5 at a time and place a wet towel over the tortillas for 10 seconds.
4. Put 3 Oz. of pork and ¼ cup of cheese in the tortilla. Firmly roll up the tortillas.
5. Line tortillas on an oiled foil pan. Spray cooking spray over tortillas.
6. Air-fry for 10 minutes. Flip over to the other side half way.
7. Serve and enjoy!!!

Air-Fried Pork Chops

Preparation Time: 10 minutes
Cook Time: 10 minutes
Total Time: 20 minutes
Serves: 4
Calories: 263 kcal

Ingredients

- ½ Tsp. salt
- ½ Cup of Dijon mustard
- 4 Pork loin chops
- 1 Cup of Italian bread crumbs
- ½ Tsp. black pepper
- ¼ Tsp. cayenne pepper

Cooking Instruction:

1. Preheat the Air Fryer to 360ºF.
2. Sprinkle the mustard on both sides of the pork chops.
3. Mix the bread crumbs, cayenne, black pepper, and salt in a small bowl.
4. Coat the pork chops in the crumbs so both sides are well dredge.
5. Put the pork chops on the Air fryer and Air-fry for 10 minutes. Flip halfway to the other sides.
6. Serve and enjoy!!!

Crispy Breaded Pork Chops

Preparation Time: 10 minutes
Cook Time: 10 minutes
Total Time: 15 minutes
Serves: 4
Calories: 368 kcal

Ingredients:

- Olive oil spray
- ½ Cup of panko crumbs
- ¼ Tsp. chili powder
- 1/8 Tsp. black pepper
- 1/3 Cup of crushed cornflakes crumbs
- 2 Tbsp. grated parmesan cheese
- Kosher salt
- 1 Large egg, beaten
- 1 ¼ Tsp. sweet paprika
- ½ Tsp. garlic powder
- 6 Centre cut boneless pork chops
- ½ Tsp. onion powder

Cooking Instructions:

1. Preheat the Air Fryer to 400ºF for about 12 minutes and put oil into it.
2. Season both sides of the pork chops with ½ Tsp. kosher salt.
3. Combine together in a big bowl - cornflake crumbs, parmesan cheese, panko, 3/4 Tsp. kosher salt, paprika, chili powder, black pepper, garlic powder and onion powder.
4. In another mixing bowl, put the beaten egg. Bury the pork into the egg and crumb mixture one after the other. Add 3 chops and sprinkle with oil.
5. Air-fry for 12 minutes. At half way, turn to the other side and air-fry for about 6 minutes. Do the same on the remaining chops.
6. Serve and enjoy!!!

Stromboli

Preparation Time: 10 minutes
Cook Time: 15 minutes
Total Time: 25 minutes
Serves: 4

Ingredients:

- 1 Egg yolk
- 1 Tbsp. milk
- 12 Oz. pizza crust, refrigerated
- 3 Cup of cheddar cheese, shredded
- 0.333333 Lbs. cooked ham, sliced
- 3 Oz. red bell peppers, roasted
- 0.75 Cup of Mozzarella cheese, shredded

Cooking Instructions:

1. Roll the dough into ¼ inch thickness.
2. On one side of the dough, pour the cheese, the ham and peppers and cover the dough. Whisk the milk and egg together.
3. Dip the dough into the egg mixture; put them into the Air Fryer and air-fry for 15 minutes.
4. At half way, turn to the other side and air-fry for about 6 minutes.
5. Serve and enjoy!!!

Beef Empanadas

Preparation Time: 10 minutes
Cook Time: 16 minutes
Total Time: 26 minutes
Serves: 4
Calories: 183

Ingredients:
- 1 Egg white, whisked
- 1 Tsp. water
- 8 Goya empanada discs, thawed
- 1 Cup of picadillo

Cooking Instructions:
1. Preheat the Air Fryer to 325ºF for 8 minutes. Pour cooking oil into the Air Fryer basket.
2. In the centre of each disc, add Tbsp. of picadillo. Fold the dough into half and make sure you cover the endings.
3. Do these steps for all the dough that is remaining. Mix water with the egg whites and then rub oil on the top of the empanadas.
4. Put them into the Air Fryer and air-fry for about 8 minutes. Repeat these to all the remaining empanadas.
5. Serve and enjoy!!!

Air Fryer Burgers

Preparation Time: 14 minutes
Cook Time: 45 minutes
Total Time: 59 minutes
Serves: 4

Ingredients:

- 1 Tsp. Garlic Puree
- 1 Tsp. Tomato Puree
- 300g Mixed Mince pork and beef
- Onion
- Salt and Pepper
- 1 Tsp. Mustard
- 4 Bread Buns
- Salad
- 1 Tsp. Basil
- 1 Tsp. Mixed Herbs
- 25g Cheddar Cheese

Cooking Instructions:

1. Mix properly all the seasonings in a mixing bowl.
2. Make them into 4 small size burgers and add them into the Air Fryer basket.
3. Air-fry at 200ºC for 25 minutes. At half way, turn to the other side and air-fry at 180ºC for about 20 minutes.
4. Top with add your salad, cheese and bun.
5. Serve and enjoy!!!

Roasted Stuffed Peppers

Preparation Time: 10 minutes
Cook Time: 15 minutes
Total Time: 25 minutes
Serves: 3

Ingredients:

- 1 Tsp. olive oil
- 8 Oz. lean ground beef
- 1 Clove garlic, minced
- ½ Tsp. black pepper
- 4 Oz. cheddar cheese, shredded
- ½ Cup of tomato sauce
- 1 Tsp. Worcestershire sauce
- ½ Tsp. salt
- 2 Medium green peppers, stems and seeds removed
- ½ Medium onion, chopped

Cooking Instructions:

1. Preheat your Air Fryer to 390°F.
2. Air-fry the garlic and onion using olive oil in a small non-stick skillet. Remove and set aside for it to cool.
3. In a large mixing bowl, mix together the cooked vegetables, beef, ¼ cup tomato sauce, salt, pepper, half the shredded cheese and Worcestershire.
4. Share and stuff the pepper halves and pour the remaining tomato sauce and cheese.
5. Put them into Air Fryer and Air-fry for about 15 minutes.
6. Serve and enjoy!!!

Rib Eye Steak

Preparation Time: 10 minutes
Cook Time: 24 minutes
Total Time: 34 minutes
Serves: 4

Ingredients:

- 2 Lbs. rib eye steak
- 1 Tbsp. olive oil
- 1 Tbsp. steak rub

Cooking Instructions:

1. Preheat your Air Fryer to 400°F.
2. Pour Olive oil into the Air Fryer and season both side of the steak.
3. Add the steak into the Air Fry basket and Air-fry at 400°F for 14 minutes. Turn the steak over to the other side after 7 minutes.
4. Remove the steak from heat and allow it to cool for about 10 minutes.
5. Serve and enjoy!!!

Country Fried Steak

Preparation Time: 10 minutes
Cook Time: 12 minutes
Total Time: 24 minutes
Serves: 1

Ingredients:

- 6 Oz. sirloin steak-pounded thin
- 3 Eggs, beaten
- 1 Cup of flour
- 1 Cup of Panko
- 1 Tsp. onion powder
- 2 Cup of milk
- 1 Tsp. pepper
- 1 Tsp. Garlic powder
- 1 Tsp. salt
- 1 Tsp. pepper
- 6 Oz. ground sausage meat
- 2 Tbsp. flour

Cooking Instructions:

1. Use all the spices to season the panko.
2. Coat the steak with flour, egg and seasoned panko.
3. Put the steak into Air Fryer basket and Air-fry at 370ºF for 12 minutes.
4. Remove the steak and allow it to cool.
5. Serve and enjoy!!!

Spicy Stuffed Peppers

Preparation Time: 20 minutes
Cook Time: 20 minutes
Total Time: 40 minutes
Serves: 4

Ingredients:
- 2 Medium potatoes, boiled and mashed
- 8 Banana peppers
- 1 Tsp. light cooking oil
- 1 Medium onion, finely chopped
- ½ Tsp. turmeric powder
- ½ Tsp. anchor powder
- Salt
- ½ Tsp. red chilli powder
- 1 Tsp. coriander powder
- 2 Tbsp. finely chopped coriander leaves

Cooking Instructions:
1. Combine together the chopped coriander leaves, mash potatoes with the onion, spices, salt.
2. Slot in each pepper in the middle and take out the seeds and ribs.
3. Each of the hollowed out pepper should be fill with equal portions of the potato mixture.
4. Preheat your Air Fryer to 180°C. Pour little oil on the pepper and place the stuffed peppers on a foiled surface.
5. Air-fry at 180°C for 7 minutes.
6. Serve and enjoy!!!

Taco Bell Crunch wrap

Preparation Time: 15 minutes
Cook Time: 4 minutes
Total Time: 19 minutes
Serves: 6

Ingredients:

- 2 Lbs. ground beef
- 2 Servings Homemade Taco Seasoning
- 6 Tostadas
- Olive oil
- 3 Roma tomatoes
- 12 Oz. nacho cheese
- 2 Cup of Lettuce, shredded
- 2 Cup of Mexican blend cheese
- 2 Cup of Sour cream
- 1 1/3 Cup of Water
- 6 Flour tortillas, 12 inch

Cooking Instructions:

1. Preheat your Air Fryer to 400ºF. Follow the taco seasoning packet and make your ground beef.
2. Mix together 2/3 cup of beef, flour tortilla, 4 tbsp. of nacho cheese, 1/3 cup of cheese, 1 tostada, 1/3 cup of sour cream, 1/3 cup of lettuce and 1/6th of the tomatoes.
3. Flood all the edges. Do these for the remaining wraps. Place them in the Air Fryer and sprinkle with olive oil.
4. Air-fry for 2 minutes. At half way, turn them over and cook for more 2 minutes.
5. Serve and enjoy!!!

Roast Beef

Preparation Time: 5 minutes
Cook Time: 45 minutes
Total Time: 50 minutes
Serves: 6
Calories: 320 kcal

Ingredients:

- 1 Tsp. salt
- 1 Tsp. rosemary
- 2 Lbs. beef roast
- 1 Tbsp. olive oil

Cooking Instructions:

1. Preheat Air Fryer to 360°F.
2. Combine sea salt, rosemary and oil on a small bowl. Put beef on bowl and stir so that the oil-herb mixes to dredge the outside.
3. Put beef in Air Fryer basket. Air-fry for 45 minutes.
4. Remove roast beef from Air Fryer, cover with a foil and allow it to cool for 10 minutes.
5. Serve and enjoy!!!

Beef Stir Fry with Homemade Marinade

Preparation Time: 20 minutes
Cook Time: 13 minutes
Total Time: 20 minutes
Serves: 4

Ingredients:

- 1 Yellow pepper
- ½ Cup of onion
- ½ Cup of red onion
- 1 Lbs. of beef sirloin
- 1½ Lbs. of broccoli florets
- 1 Red pepper
- 1 Green pepper

Sauce and Marinade:

- 1 Tbsp. of soy sauce
- 1 Tsp. of ground ginger
- ¼ Cup of water
- ¼ Cup of hoisin sauce
- 2 Tsp. of minced garlic
- 1 Tsp. of sesame oil

Cooking Instructions:

1. Mix all the ingredients for the sauce and marinate to a bowl, then put the meat.
2. Put in the freezer for about 20 minutes. Put 1 Tbsp. of stir fryer oil, and combine it with the vegetables.
3. Put your vegetables in the Air Fryer basket, and Air-fry for about 5 minutes at 200ºF. Open your Air Fryer, combine all of the vegetables.
4. If hard, Air-fry for another 2 minutes. Remove the vegetables and put them in a bowl, then put your meat in the Air Fryer basket.
5. Air-fry for 4 minutes at 360ºF. Turn them and Air-fry for another 2 minutes if they aren't done.
6. Serve and enjoy!!!

BBQ Ribs

Preparation Time: 20 minutes
Cook Time: 13 minutes
Total Time: 20 minutes
Serves: 4

Ingredients:

- 32 Oz. BBQ sauce
- 3 Lbs. baby back ribs
- Salt and pepper

Cooking Instructions:

1. Preheat your Air Fryer to 390°F.
2. Add salt and pepper to the ribs. Remove the membrane.
3. Dip your ribs in BBQ sauce and put them in your Air Fryer basket.
4. Air-fry for 10 minutes. Turn them and Air-fry for another 7 minutes.
5. Remove from Air Fryer, put additional sauce.
6. Serve and enjoy!!!

Mongolian Beef

Preparation Time: 20 minutes
Cook Time: 20 minutes
Total Time: 40 minutes
Serves: 4
Ingredients:
Meat:
- ¼ Cup of Corn Starch
- 1 Lbs. Flank Steak

Sauce:
- ½ Tsp. Ginger
- 1 Tbsp. Minced Garlic
- ½ Cup of Soy Sauce or Gluten Free Soy Sauce
- 2 Tsp. Vegetable Oil
- ½ Cup of Water
- ¾ Cup of Brown Sugar Packed

Optional: Cooked Rice, green Beans and green Onions
Cooking Instructions:
1. Chop thinly the steak in long pieces and then dredge with the corn starch.
2. Put in the Air Fryer and Air-fry on 390°F for 10 minutes on both side.
3. While cooking the steak, warm the sauce ingredient in a saucepan on medium-high heat. Mix the ingredients together until it boils lowly.
4. Put the steak in a bowl with the sauce when it is done and let it coat for about 10 minutes.
5. Use tongs to remove the steak and shake off excess sauce when it is ready. Add steak on cooked rice and green beans.
6. Serve and enjoy!!!

Honey Mustard Pork Chops

Preparation Time: 5 minutes
Cook Time: 8 minutes
Total Time: 13 minutes
Serves: 4

Ingredients:

- 4 Pork chops ½ inch thick
- 4 Tbsp. mustard
- 2 Tbsp. honey
- 2 Tbsp. minced garlic
- 1 Tsp. salt
- 1 Tsp. pepper
- Oil to spray chops

Cooking Instructions:

1. Combine together mustard, salt, garlic, honey, and pepper in a big bowl.
2. Put the pork chops and throw to dredge with the sauce.
3. Grease the Air Fryer basket. Put the chops into the greased basket.
4. Air-fry for 12 minutes at 350°F. Turn half way and grease with oil again.
5. Serve and enjoy!!!

Sausage Rolls

Preparation Time: 5 minutes
Cook Time: 10 minutes
Total Time: 15 minutes
Serves: 4
Calories: 149 kcal

Ingredients:

- 1 Small Egg Beaten
- 2 Tsp. Thyme
- Salt & Pepper
- 2.5 Weight Watchers Wraps
- 200 g Minced Pork

Cooking Instructions:

1. Combine together the minced pork and the seasonings in a bowl.
2. Use your hands to mix. Shape it into a sausage meat roll and refrigerate it for 10 minutes.
3. Keep a Weight Watchers Wrap onto a clean work surface. Rub it with beaten egg.
4. Put the filling in the centre and roll it up. Cover with eggs and Air-fry for 5 minutes on both sides in the Air Fryer at 400°F.
5. Serve and enjoy!!!

AIR FRYER MAIN MEAL RECIPES

Stir Fried Zoodles and Vegetables with Tofu

Preparation Time: 20 minutes
Cook Time: 15 minutes
Total Time: 35 minutes
Serves: 4

Ingredients:

- 2 Tbsp. brown rice syrup or honey
- 2 Tbsp. sriracha chili sauce
- 8 Oz. spiralized zucchini (zoodles)
- Fresh cilantro leaves
- 2 Carrots, sliced
- 1 Red bell pepper, sliced
- 2 Tbsp. soy sauce
- 1 Tbsp. sesame oil
- 1 Tsp. minced fresh ginger
- 1 Lb. extra firm tofu, cubed
- ½ Onion, sliced
- 1 Cup of snow peas, sliced lengthwise
- 1 Tbsp. canola oil
- 2 Tbsp. rice wine vinegar
- 1 Can baby corn, drained

Cooking Instructions:

1. Mix together the brown rice syrup, canola oil, rice wine vinegar, ginger, soy sauce, sesame oil, sriracha chili sauce and tofu in a small mixing bowl.
2. Allow the mixture to absorb for 15 minutes. Preheat your Air Fryer to 360ºF. Get the tofu cubes out from the absorbed mixture and place them on a clean paper towel to dry.
3. Coat the bottom of your Air Fryer with enough oil. Air-fry the tofu for about 10 minutes and set it aside when it is done.
4. Toss in onion and carrots to the pan and Air-fry for a few minutes. Toss in the snow peas, red pepper, and baby corn and continue to Air-fry for about 5 minutes.
5. As they are still cooking, put the zucchini noodles and zoodles. After 2 minutes, get the tofu back to the pan and put the absorbed mixture.
6. Air-fry for about 3 more minutes. Top with fresh cilantro leaves.
7. Serve and enjoy!!!

Jalapeno Poppers

Preparation Time: 10 minutes
Cook Time: 8 minutes
Total Time: 18 minutes
Serves: 3

Ingredients:
- 3/4 Cup of gluten-free tortilla or bread crumbs
- 8 Oz. of cream cheese
- ¼ Cup of fresh parsley
- 10 Jalapeno peppers halved and deseeded

Cooking Instructions:
1. Combine together ½ of cream cheese and crumbs.
2. Put Parsley and dip each pepper into the mixture.
3. To make the top coating on the pepper, press the tops of the peppers into the remaining ¼ cup of crumbs.
4. Air-fry at 370ºF for 8 minutes.
5. Serve and enjoy!!!

Deep Dish Prosciutto, Spinach & Mushroom Pizza

Preparation Time: 20 minutes
Cook Time: 35 minutes
Total Time: 55 minutes
Serves: 4

Ingredients:

- 2 Cups of grated mozzarella cheese
- 4 Oz. thinly sliced prosciutto
- 4 Oz. button mushrooms, sliced
- ¾ Cup of frozen spinach, thawed
- 1 Lb. pizza dough, homemade and thawed
- 1 Tbsp. olive oil
- ¼ Tsp. Italian seasoning
- 1½ Cups of pizza sauce

Cooking Instructions:

1. Add the mushrooms into the olive oil and Italian seasoning. Keep aside to absorb for about 15 minutes.
2. Squeeze water out from the spinach and also keep it aside. Preheat Air Fryer to 450°F. Pour oil into the cooking pan.
3. Prepare the pizza dough into a circle that is 11 inches and put them into the cooking pan. Stuff inside of the pizza crust with the sauce.
4. Add half of the mozzarella cheese on the top. Pour half of the spinach and mushrooms over the cheese. (Repeat this step).
5. Cut the prosciutto up into small pieces and spread the pieces on top of the pizza. Keep the pan in the Air-fryer.
6. Air-fryer at 450°F for 35 minutes. Top with salad.
7. Serve and enjoy!!!

Cauliflower Pan Pizza

Preparation Time: 10 minutes
Cook Time: 20 minutes
Total Time: 30 minutes
Serves: 2

Ingredients:

- 2 Tbsp. flour
- 1 Egg
- ⅓ Cup of Parmesan cheese
- ¼ Cup of pizza sauce
- Fresh basil leaves
- 1½ Cups of grated mozzarella cheese, divided
- 2 Cups of grated cauliflower
- ½ Tsp. oregano
- Salt
- Freshly ground black pepper

Cooking Instructions:

1. Preheat the Air Fryer to 400°F.
2. Chop your cauliflower in a food processor. Squeeze all the water out from the cauliflower and put the cauliflower in a large bowl.
3. Put oregano, flour, egg, parmesan cheese, salt, ½ cup of the mozzarella cheese, and pepper. Mix thoroughly.
4. Place aluminium foil into the baking pan and pour the cauliflower mixture into the pan. Air-fry for 10 minutes.
5. Get the pan out from Air Fryer and turn the cauliflower onto a plate. Air-fry the bottom of the crust at 400°F for 5 minutes.
6. Keep the foil and crust back into the baking pan. Sprinkle the remaining mozzarella cheese, pizza sauce and some dried oregano on the crust.
7. Air-fry the pizza at 360°F for 5 minutes. When the pizza is done, allow it to cool in the air fryer for some few minutes.
8. Remove the pizza from the pan and top with fresh basil.
9. Serve and enjoy!!!

Spicy Black Bean Turkey Burgers with Cumin-Avocado Spread

Preparation Time: 10 minutes
Cook Time: 21 minutes
Total Time: 31 minutes
Serves 2

Ingredients:
- 2 Tbsp. minced red onion
- 1 Tbsp. chopped fresh cilantro
- Freshly ground black pepper
- 1 Jalapeño pepper, seeded and minced
- 2 Tbsp. plain breadcrumbs
- 1 Cup of canned black beans, drained and rinsed
- ¾ Lb. ground turkey
- ½ Tsp. salt
- ½ Tsp. chili powder
- ¼ Tsp. cayenne pepper
- Olive or vegetable oil
- 1 Ripe avocado
- Juice of 1 lime
- 1 Tsp. ground cumin
- 2 Slices pepper Jack cheese
- Toasted burger rolls, sliced tomatoes, lettuce leaves

Cooking Instructions:
1. Put the black beans in a large mixing bowl and put red onion, chili powder, Jalapeño pepper, breadcrumbs, ground turkey, salt and cayenne pepper.
2. Mix them thoroughly and make them into the shape of 2 patties and rub both sides with olive oil. Pre-heat the air fryer to 380°F.
3. Place the burgers into the Air Fryer basket and Air-fry for 20 minutes. At half way, turn them over to the other side and cook. Top with the pepper Jack cheese.
4. To make the cumin avocado spread, put the cumin, avocado, salt and lime juice in food processor and process until smooth.
5. Pour in freshly ground black pepper and season with the cilantro. Remove the burgers from the Air Fryer when they are properly cooked and rub olive oil on inside of the burgers.
6. Keep the burger into the Air Fryer and Air-fry at 400°F for 1 minute. Sprinkle the cumin-avocado spread on the burgers and make your burgers with lettuce and sliced tomatoes.
7. Serve and enjoy!!!

Lemon-Dill Salmon Burgers

Preparation Time: 10 minutes
Cook Time: 8 minutes
Total Time: 18 minutes
Serves 4

Ingredients:
- Freshly ground black pepper
- 2 Eggs, lightly beaten
- 2 (6 Oz.) Fillets of salmon, finely chopped
- 2 Tbsp. chopped fresh dill weed
- 1 Tsp. salt
- 1 Cup of fine breadcrumbs
- 1 Tsp. freshly grated lemon zest

Instructions:
1. Preheat the Air Fryer to 400°F. Mix all the ingredients in a mixing bowl and make them into 4 balls.
2. Make the balls to be flattened and use your thumb to press the centre of the patty.
3. Place the burgers into the Air Fryer basket and Air-fry for 4 minutes. Half way while it cooks turn them over and air-fry for another 4 minutes.
4. Top with tomato, red onion, lettuce or avocado.

General Tso's Cauliflower

Preparation Time: 10 minutes
Cook Time: 15 minutes
Total Time: 25 minutes
Serves 2

Ingredients:

- 1 Head cauliflower cut in florets

- Steamed broccoli

- 3 Eggs

- 1 Cup of panko breadcrumbs

- Canola or peanut oil, in a spray bottle

- 2 Tbsp. oyster sauce

- 2 Tbsp. rice wine vinegar

- 2 Tbsp. sugar

- ¾ Cup of all-purpose flour, divided

- White or brown rice for serving

- ¼ Cup of water

- ¼ Cup of soy sauce

- 2 Tsp. chili paste

Cooking Instructions:

1. Using 3 bowls, prepare a dredging station. In the first bowl, put the cauliflower and pour ¼ cup of the flour on the top.
2. In the second bowl, put the eggs and in the third bowl, mix the panko breadcrumbs and remaining ½ cup flour.
3. Toss in cauliflower into the flour for proper coating of the florets. Burys the cauliflower florets in the eggs.
4. Dip them into the breadcrumbs for proper coating. Keep the cauliflower florets on a baking pan and sprinkle with peanut oil or canola.
5. Preheat the Air Fryer to 400°F. Air-fry at 400°F for 15 minutes. Half way while it cooks turn them over and Air-fry for another 5 minutes. Spray with more oil.
6. Prepare the General Tso Sauce by mixing the soy sauce, chili paste, oyster sauce, rice wine vinegar, sugar and water in a saucepan and boil them.
7. When the Air Fryer cooking time completes, turn the cauliflower onto a serving plate and sprinkle with the sauce.
8. Serve and enjoy!!!

Curry Chickpeas

Preparation Time: 10 minutes
Cook Time: 15 minutes
Total Time: 25 minutes
Serves 2

Ingredients:

- 1/8 Tsp. ground cinnamon
- ¼ Tsp. kosher salt
- 2 Tsp. curry powder
- ½ Tsp. ground turmeric
- ¼ Tsp. ground cumin
- ¼ Tsp. plus
- 1 (15 Oz.) Can no-salt-added chickpeas, drained and rinsed
- 2 Tbsp. red wine vinegar
- 2 Tbsp. olive oil
- ½ Tsp. Aleppo pepper Thinly sliced fresh cilantro
- ¼ Tsp. ground coriander

Cooking Instructions:

1. Hit chickpeas with your hands lightly in a medium bowl. Put vinegar, oil, curry powder, cumin, turmeric, coriander and cinnamon. Mix thoroughly.
2. Put the chickpeas in Air Fryer basket and Air-fry at 400°F for about 15 minutes. Half way while it cooks turn them over and continue cooking.
3. Turn the chickpeas to a serving bowl and sprinkle with cilantro, salt and Aleppo pepper.
4. Serve and enjoy!!!

Chicken Wing Drumettes

Preparation Time: 15 minutes
Cook Time: 36 minutes
Total Time: 25 minutes
Serves 2

Ingredients:

- 3 Tbsp. honey
- 10 Large chicken drumettes
- Cooking spray
- 2 Tbsp. chopped unsalted roasted peanuts
- 1 Tbsp. chopped fresh chives
- ¼ Cup of rice vinegar
- 2 Tbsp. unsalted chicken stock
- 3/8 Tsp. crushed red pepper
- 1 Garlic clove, finely chopped
- 1 Tbsp. lower-sodium soy sauce
- 1 Tbsp. toasted sesame oil

Cooking Instructions:

1. Keep chicken into the Air Fryer basket and sprinkle with cooking oil.
2. Air-fry at 400°F for 30 minutes. Half way while it cooks turn them over and continue cooking.
3. In a small bowl, mix together vinegar, crushed red pepper, stock, soy sauce, honey, oil, and garlic.
4. Air-fry for about 6 minutes. Put drumettes in a medium bowl. Put the vinegar mixture and sprinkle with chives and peanuts.
5. Serve and enjoy!!!

Turkey Breast with Cherry Glaze

Preparation Time: 10 minutes
Cook Time: 54 minutes
Total Time: 1 hour 4 minutes
Serves 7

Ingredients:

- 1 (5 Lbs.) Turkey breast
- 1 Tsp. soy sauce
- Freshly ground black pepper
- ½ Tsp. dried sage
- 1 Tsp. salt
- ½ Tsp. freshly ground black pepper
- ½ Cup of cherry preserves
- 2 Tsp. olive oil
- 1 Tsp. dried thyme
- 1 Tbsp. chopped fresh thyme leaves

Cooking Instructions:

1. Preheat the Air Fryer to 350°F. Rub olive oil on the turkey breast.
2. Mix together the sage, thyme, salt and pepper and brush the spice mixture on outside of the turkey breast.
3. Put the seasoned turkey breast into the Air Fryer basket and Air-fry at 350°F for 25 minutes.
4. Move the turkey breast on its side and Air-fry for another 12 minutes. Flip them to the other side and Air-fry for another 12 minutes.
5. Mix together the soy sauce, cherry preserves, fresh thyme, and pepper in a small mixing bowl.
6. When the turkey breast is well cooked, rub the glaze all over the turkey. Air-fry for another 5 minutes.
7. Serve and enjoy!!!

Quick Roasted Tomato Sauce with Capers and Basil

Preparation Time: 10 minutes
Cook Time: 20 minutes
Total Time: 30 minutes
Serves 4

Ingredients:

- 1½ Pints cherry tomatoes, halved
- ¼ Cup of chopped fresh basil
- Grated Parmesan cheese
- 2 Tbsp. capers
- 1 Tsp. Italian seasoning
- 2 Tbsp. olive oil
- 1 Tbsp. white wine vinegar
- 1 Clove garlic, minced
- 1 Shallot, diced
- ½ Lb. dried pasta, cooked

Cooking Instructions:

1. Preheat the Air Fryer to 400°F.
2. Mix together the Italian seasoning, olive oil, white wine vinegar, garlic, shallots, cherry tomatoes, capers, salt and freshly ground black pepper in a small mixing bowl.
3. Flip the mixture to the Air Fryer basket. Air-fry for 20 minutes and shake the basket occasionally while it's still cooking.
4. Bury the pasta into the tomato sauce. Pour fresh basil, salt and freshly ground black pepper.
5. Serve and enjoy!!!

Salt and Pepper Filets Mignon with Horseradish Cream Sauce

Preparation Time: 10 minutes
Cook Time: 15 minutes
Total Time: 25 minutes
Serves 4
Ingredients:
- 4 (8 Oz.) filets mignons
- 1 Tsp. chopped fresh thyme
- 1 Tbsp. chopped fresh parsley
- 2 Tbsp. lemon juice
- 3 Tbsp. prepared horseradish
- ¾ Cup of crème fraîche
- coarse salt and coarsely ground black pepper

Cooking Instructions:
1. Preheat the Air Fryer to 400°F.
2. Use freshly ground black pepper and salt to season the steak and turn them into the Air Fryer.
3. Air-fry for 15 minutes. At half way while cooking, turn them over. When cooking time is up, get the steaks out from the Air Fryer.
4. Allow them cool for 5 minutes. While the steaks are cooling, make the horseradish cream.
5. Mix together the horseradish, lemon juice, parsley, crème fraiche, thyme, salt and freshly ground black pepper in a small bowl. Top with horseradish sauce.
6. Serve and enjoy!!!

Peach, Prosciutto and Burrata Flatbread

Preparation Time: 10 minutes
Cook Time: 14 minutes
Total Time: 24 minutes
Serves 2

Ingredients:

- 3 Slices thinly sliced serrano ham
- Olive oil
- 1 Peach, pitted and sliced
- 1 Tbsp. butter, melted
- Balsamic glaze
- Mint leaves, chopped
- 2 Tbsp. dark brown sugar
- 1 Pre-made 7-inch naan bread
- 2 Oz. burrata cheese

Cooking Instructions:

1. Rub melted butter on both sides of the peach slices. Put them into the Air Fryer basket and put dark brown sugar.
2. Preheat the Air Fryer to 400°F. Air-fry for 5 minutes and then flip them to a plate and keep aside.
3. Sprinkle olive oil in the Air Fryer and put the ham in the Air Fryer basket. Air-fry at 400°F for 2 minutes and then turn them onto the same plate with the peaches.
4. Rub olive oil on both sides of the naan bread. Air-fry at 400°F for 3 minutes. Turn the bread to the other side.
5. Air-fry for 2 minutes. Pour the prepared peaches and ham on top of the bread. Put dollops of burrata and Air-fry at 370°F for 2 minutes.
6. Remove the flatbread into a platter and sprinkle balsamic glaze, coarsely chopped mint leaves and season with freshly ground black pepper.
7. Serve and enjoy!!!

Inside Out Cheeseburgers

Preparation Time: 8 minutes
Cook Time: 20 minutes
Total Time: 28 minutes
Serves: 2

Ingredients:

- 2 Tsp. yellow mustard
- Salt and freshly ground black pepper
- 12 Oz. lean ground beef
- 3 Tbsp. minced onion
- 4 Tsp. ketchup
- 8 Hamburger dill pickle chips
- 4 Slices of Cheddar cheese

Cooking Instructions:

1. Mix together minced onion, ketchup, salt, ground beef, mustard and pepper in a large bowl and shred the meat into four equal parts.
2. For stuffed burgers, cut each portion of the meat into a small thin patty. On the centre of two patties, put half of the cheese and 4 pickle chips and keep a rim around the edge of the patty exposed.
3. Get the other two patties and keep them on top the first and press the meat together and cover the edges.
4. Keep the burger on a workable flat surface and use your hand to make a straight edge. Preheat the Air Fryer to 370°F.
5. Keep the burgers in the Air Fryer basket and Air-fry for 20 minutes. Half way while cooking, turn the burgers over and continue cooking. Top with tomato.
6. Serve and enjoy!!!

Roasted Vegetable Pasta Salad

Preparation Time: 10 minutes
Cook Time: 14 minutes
Total Time: 24 minutes
Serves: 7

Ingredients:

- 1 Red pepper, large chunks
- ¼ Cup of olive oil
- 2 Tbsp. chopped fresh basil
- 1 Zucchini, sliced into half
- 1 Yellow squash, sliced into half
- 1 Red onion, sliced
- 4 Oz. brown mushrooms, halved
- 1 Orange pepper, large chunks
- 1 Green pepper, large chunks
- 1 Lb. penne rigate or rigatoni, cooked
- 1 Cup of grape tomatoes, halved
- ½ Cup of pitted Kalamata olives, halved
- 3 Tbsp. balsamic vinegar
- 1 Tsp. Italian seasoning
- Salt and fresh ground black pepper

Cooking Instructions:

1. Preheat the Air Fryer to 380°F.
2. In a large mixing bowl, mix together the zucchini, mushrooms, yellow squash, peppers and red onion.
3. Pour a small olive oil and mix them thoroughly for proper coating. Season with salt and pepper. Put the Italian seasoning and Air-fry for 14 Half way while still cooking, shake the Air-fryer for proper cooking.
4. In another large mixing bowl, mix together the roasted vegetables, tomatoes, cooked pasta, olives and balsamic vinegar.
5. Toss; put more olive oil, season with salt and freshly ground black pepper. Put the salad on the refrigerator.
6. Serve and enjoy!!!

AIR FRYER EGG RECIPES

Scotch Eggs

Preparation Time: 30 minutes
Cook Time: 15 minutes
Total Time: 45 minutes
Serves: 6

Ingredients:
- 2 Cloves garlic, minced
- 1 ½ Cups of panko bread crumbs
- 1 Tsp. snipped fresh thyme
- 1 Tsp. salt
- 2 Tsp. lemon juice
- 6 Cups of arugula
- 1 Tsp. pepper
- 1/2 Tsp. snipped fresh sage
- 1 Lb. ground pork
- ½ Cup of all-purpose flour
- 2 Eggs
- 1/3 Cup of finely chopped onion
- 1 Tbsp. snipped fresh chives
- 2 Tbsp. water
- 6 Eggs, hard-cooked, peeled
- ½ Cup of mayonnaise
- 1 - 2 Tbsp. Sriracha sauce

Cooking Instructions:
1. Preheat Air Fryer to 350ºF. Mix together 1 clove garlic, thyme, ½ Tsp pepper, onion, chives, ½ Tsp. salt, sage and ground pork in a large mixing bowl.
2. Mix together the remaining ½ Tsp. flour, salt and pepper. Break the 2 eggs and put water in another bowl. In a different mixing bowl put panko.
3. Bury each cooked egg in the flour mixture. Share the meat mixture into six places. Make them into flat-thin patties and fold around hard cooked eggs.
4. Cover and smooth the edges. Work with and egg at a time, bury the egg into the flour and beaten eggs and roll in panko.
5. Put the eggs in the Air Fryer basket. Air-fry for 15 minutes. Mix together Sriracha, remaining 1 clove garlic, lemon juice and mayonnaise in a small mixing bowl.
6. Top with spicy Mayonnaise.
7. Serve and enjoy!!!

Scratch Scotch Eggs

Preparation Time: 30 minutes
Cook Time: 30 minutes
Total Time: 1 hour
Serves: 6
Ingredients:
- ¹/₃ Cup of finely chopped onion
- 1 Tbsp. snipped fresh chives
- 1 Tsp. dried sage, crushed
- 3/4 Tsp. sea salt
- 3/4 Tsp. black pepper
- 1/2 Tsp. dried thyme, crushed
- 2 Tbsp. poppy seeds
- 6 Cups fresh spinach
- 6 Eggs, hard cooked and peeled
- ¹/₃ Cup of almond meal
- ½ Cup of Aioli
- 1 Lb. ground pork

Cooking Instructions:
1. Preheat the Air Fryer to 350ºF.
2. Place aluminium foil in a baking pan. Mix together onions, fresh chives, sage, black pepper, thyme and ground pork.
3. Share the prepared meat mixture into six places. Make them into flat-thin patties and fold around hard cooked eggs. Cover and smooth the edges.
4. In a small mixing bowl, mix together the poppy seeds and almonds. Dip the eggs into almond mixture. Keep them on the baking pan.
5. Air-fry for 30 minutes.
6. Serve and enjoy!!!

Eggs Benedict

Preparation Time: 10 minutes
Cook Time: 8 minutes
Total Time: 18 minutes
Serves: 6

Ingredients:

- 2 English Muffins split
- 4 Slices of Canadian-style bacon
- 4 Eggs

Cooking Instructions:

1. Pour cooking oil in your baking pan.
2. Fill half of the skillet with water. Boil the water. In a small mixing bowl, beat one of the eggs.
3. Pour the egg into the boiling water and put the remaining eggs one after the other. Boil the eggs uncovered for about 5 minutes.
4. Put water into a large pan or bowl and remove the eggs into it. On a baking pan, cut the muffins into half and keep on the pan. Boil for about 2 minutes.
5. Place Canadian-style bacon on the muffin halves. Boil for about 1 minute. Top each bacon-topped muffin half with an egg.
6. Serve and enjoy!!!

Smoked Salmon Eggs Benedict

Preparation Time: 10 minutes
Cook Time: 8 minutes
Total Time: 18 minutes
Serves: 4

Ingredients:

- ¼ Cup of light sour cream
- 1 Tsp. lemon juice
- 1 Tsp. dry mustard
- 4 Tsp. fat-free milk
- 8 Eggs
- 4 Whole wheat English muffins, split and toasted
- 4 Oz. thinly sliced smoked salmon
- Ground black pepper

Cooking Instructions:

1. Mix together lemon juice, sour cream, dry mustard and enough milk.
2. Keep aside. Put oil into baking pan and keep the poacher cups on boiling water. Beat one of the eggs into a measuring cup and slide egg into a poacher cup.
3. Do this for the remaining eggs. Air-fry for about 8 minutes. Roll a knife on the edges to enable loosen eggs.
4. Turn the poacher cups upside down to enable you remove eggs. Top with poached eggs.
5. Serve and enjoy!!!

Hard Boiled Eggs

Preparation Time: 3 minutes
Cook Time: 18 minutes
Total Time: 21 minutes
Serves: 4
Ingredients:
- 8 eggs

Cooking Instructions:
1. Preheat your Air Fryer to 260ºF.
2. Put the eggs in a bowl and cook for about 18 minutes.
3. When the cooking time is up, remove the bowl and put the eggs in cold water. Peel the shell.
4. Serve and enjoy!!!

Baked Eggs

Preparation Time: 5 minutes
Cook Time: 5 minutes
Total Time: 10 minutes
Serves: 2

Ingredients:

- non-stick cooking spray
- 2 eggs
- Salt and pepper

Cooking Instructions:

1. Preheat your Air Fryer to 180°F. Sprinkle oil on your ramekin.
2. Beat the eggs into the ramekin.
3. Put salt and pepper.
4. Air-fry at 330°F for 5 minutes.
5. Serve and enjoy!!!

Ham and Egg Pie

Preparation Time: 5 minutes
Cook Time: 52 minutes
Total Time: 57 minutes
Serves: 8

Ingredients:

- 6 Eggs, slightly beaten
- 1 Cup of cream-style cottage cheese
- 2 Cups of all-purpose flour
- 1 Tbsp. baking powder
- ½ Tsp. salt
- ½ Cup of milk
- 2 Tbsp. sliced green onion
- 2 Tbsp. snipped fresh Italian parsley
- 1/3 Cup of cooking oil
- ½ (2 Oz.) Cup of shredded sharp cheddar cheese
- 2 Oz. cooked ham, shredded
- 2 Oz. salami, shredded
- ½ (2 Oz.) Cup of shredded mozzarella cheese

Cooking Instructions:

1. Preheat Air Fryer to 350°F. Mix together baking powder, all-purpose flour and salt. In the centre of the dry ingredients, create a well in a medium bowl.
2. In a different small bowl mix together milk and oil. Put all the liquid ingredients and mix thoroughly. Spread flour on a flat surface and then pour the mixture on top.
3. Fold, press the dough and roll the dough on the floured surface into a 12-inch circle. Line up the dough on a pan and fold under the extra pastry, joining the edge as you wish.
4. Mix together shredded cheeses, eggs, ham, green onion, salami, cottage cheese, and parsley in a medium bowl and pour the mixture into unbaked crust.
5. Air-fry for 52 minutes. Allow it to cool.
6. Serve and enjoy!!!

Ham and Egg Sandwiches

Preparation Time: 10 minutes
Cook Time: 10 minutes
Total Time: 20 minutes
Serves: 4

Ingredients:

- 1 Tbsp. milk
- Ground black pepper
- 2 Hard-cooked eggs, peeled and sliced
- 4 4-Inch pieces multigrain baguette-style French bread, split
- 4 Oz. Havarti cheese, thinly sliced
- 4 Oz. shaved ham
- ¼ Cup of plain Greek yogurt
- 1 Tbsp. snipped fresh dill
- 8 Lengthwise sandwich pickle slices

Cooking Instructions:

1. Mix together 1 Tsp. dill, yogurt, milk and pepper in a small mixing bowl.
2. Spray them on one cut side of each baguette.
3. Layer with slices of ham, cheese, and pickle. Top with slices of egg.
4. Serve and enjoy!!!

Ham and Egg Salad on Toast

Preparation Time: 8 minutes
Cook Time: 10 minutes
Total Time: 18 minutes
Serves: 4

Ingredients:

- ⅓ Cup of mayonnaise
- ½ Bunch watercress, trimmed
- 1 Tbsp. Dijon-style mustard
- R6 Oz. ham, sliced
- 2 Tbsp. sweet pickle relish
- 4 Mehick slices challah, sweet Hawaiian, toasted

Cooking Instructions:

1. Preheat Air Fryer to 400°F. Rub oil on one side of each slice of bread.
2. Place them on a baking pan. Air-fry for 10 minutes.
3. Mix together the capers, parsley, shallot, chives, eggs, mustard, 2 Tbsp. olive oil, salt, lemon juice, and pepper.
4. Top with toasted bread.
5. Serve and enjoy!!!

Poached Egg Salad

Preparation Time: 10 minutes
Cook Time: 9 minutes
Total Time: 19 minutes
Serves: 4

Ingredients:

- 8 Eggs
- 2 Medium leeks, thinly sliced
- 2 Oz. blue cheese, crumbled
- Salt and ground black pepper
- 4 Slices crusty bread, toasted
- 2 Cups of seedless red grapes
- 2 Tbsp. cider vinegar
- 1 10 Oz. package Italian mixed salad greens

Cooking Instructions:

1. Fill water on a pan half way. Boil the water.
2. Beat the eggs into a cup. Take the cup and slide in egg into the pan with equal spacing.
3. Air-fry for about 5 minutes. Do not cover it.
4. In another cooking pan, put 2 Tbsp. olive oil, leeks and grapes. Air-fry for 4 minutes.
5. Remove the egg from heat, put vinegar, salt and pepper.
6. Serve and enjoy!!!

Southern Devilled Eggs

Preparation Time: 5 minutes
Cook Time: 2 minutes
Total Time: 7 minutes
Serves: 6

Ingredients:

- 3 Tbsp. mayonnaise
- 6 Eggs hard boiled
- 1 ½ Tbsp. sweet pickle relish
- Paprika and sweet baby gherkin
- 1 Tsp. mustard
- Salt and pepper

Cooking Instructions:

1. Place your hard-boiled eggs in ice water.
2. Divide the egg into two equal parts, remove the egg yolk and put in a bowl.
3. Remove the yolks on all the eggs, use a fork to mash all the yolks.
4. Put the mustard, salt, relish, mayonnaise and pepper and mix thoroughly.
5. Put the mashed yolk into a piping bag and place it into the empty white shells.
6. Put paprika and a slice of gherkin.
7. Serve and enjoy!!!

Easy Cheese Omelette

Preparation Time: 8 minutes
Cook Time: 8 minutes
Total Time: 16 minutes
Serves: 6

Ingredients:

- 2 Eggs
- Salt and pepper
- ¼ Cup of cream
- ¼ Cup of shredded cheddar cheese

Cooking Instructions:

1. Combine together eggs, cream, salt, and pepper in a small mixing bowl.
2. Mix thoroughly. Turn into a non-stick pan and put the pan into the Air Fryer. Air-fry at 350°F for 4 minutes.
3. Immediately the cooking time is up, spray your cheese on top and Air-fry at 350°F for 4 minutes.
4. Remove the pan from the Air Fryer. Flip onto a serve plate.
5. Serve and enjoy!!!

Scrambled Eggs

Preparation Time: 1 minute
Cook Time: 9 minutes
Total Time: 10 minutes
Serves: 2
Calories: 201 kcal

Ingredients:

- 4 Large Eggs
- 2 Slices Whole-meal Bread
- Salt and Pepper

Cooking Instructions:

1. Warm your bread at 400°F for 3 minutes to be hard like toast.
2. Beat your eggs into your Air Fryer. Put seasoning and keep the baking pan inside the Air Fryer.
3. Air-fry at 360°F for 2 minutes. Stir and Air-fry for another 4 minutes.
4. Sprinkle the scrambled eggs on the whole-meal.
5. Serve and enjoy!!!

Egg in Hole

Preparation Time: 5 minutes
Cook Time: 10 minutes
Total Time: 15 minutes
Serves: 1

Ingredients:

- 1 Egg
- 1 Piece of toast
- Salt and pepper

Cooking Instructions:

1. Pour cooking spray on your Air Fryer cooking pan.
2. Put your piece of bread into your Air Fryer cooking pan.
3. Create a hole using cookie cutter and remove the bread. Beat the egg into the hole.
4. Air Fry at 330°F for about 6 minutes. Flip the egg over and Air-fry for another 4 minutes.
5. Serve and enjoy!!!

Egg and Wilted Spinach Salad

Preparation Time: 30 minutes
Cook Time: 14 minutes
Total Time: 44 minutes
Serves: 4

Ingredients:

- 8 Eggs
- 1 5 Oz bag baby spinach
- 3 Tbsp. olive oil
- 2 Tbsp. balsamic vinegar
- 1 Tbsp. honey
- 4 Oz. blue cheese, crumbled
- 2 Medium Granny Smith apples, cored and sliced

Cooking Instructions:

1. Put spinach in a large mixing bowl and keep aside.
2. Put the apple slices in Air Fryer cooking pan, put 2 Tbsp. olive oil and Air-fry for 4 minutes.
3. Put honey and balsamic vinegar. Boil them, pour them into spinach and mix properly.
4. Put the remaining 1 tbsp. olive oil in Air Fryer, beat 4 eggs into the cooking pan, pour in half of the blue cheese, salt and pepper.
5. Air-fry at 205°F for 5 minutes. Do this for the remaining eggs.
6. Serve and enjoy!!!

AIR FRYER SIDE DISH RECIPES

Root Vegetable Toss with Tarragon Yogurt Dressing

Preparation Time: 10 minutes
Cook Time: 24 minutes
Total Time: 34 minutes
Serves: 2

Ingredients:
- 1 Parsnip, peeled and sliced
- 1 Small turnip, chopped
- ½ Red onion, chopped
- 1 Tsp. dried thyme
- Salt and freshly ground black pepper
- 2 Carrots, peeled and sliced on the bias
- ⅓ Lb. fingerling potatoes, halved lengthwise
- 2 Cloves garlic, halved
- 2 Tbsp. olive oil

Tarragon Yogurt Dressing:
- ½ Cup of plain yogurt
- 1 Tbsp. water
- Salt and freshly ground black pepper
- 1 Tbsp. honey
- 1 Tbsp. chopped fresh tarragon
- ½ Tbsp. olive oil
- Juice of ½ lemon
- Zest of 1 lemon

Cooking Instructions:
1. Preheat the Air Fryer to 400°F.
2. Mix together carrots, garlic, parsnip, turnip, red onion, fingerling potatoes, salt and freshly ground black pepper in a large bowl.
3. Toss the vegetables with the olive oil and dried thyme. Pour the vegetables to the Air Fryer basket and Air-fry at 400°F for 25 minutes.
4. Keep on shaking the basket until cooking time is completed. Mix together lemon juice, fresh tarragon, lemon zest, yogurt, honey, olive oil and water in a small mixing bowl.
5. Put salt and freshly ground black pepper to taste. Flip the vegetables onto a serving platter and garnish with tarragon leaves.
6. Serve and enjoy!!!

Quick Roasted Tomato Sauce with Capers and Basil

Preparation Time: 10 minutes
Cook Time: 20 minutes
Total Time: 30 minutes
Serves: 4

Ingredients:

- 1 Clove garlic, minced
- 1 Shallot, diced
- 1½ Pints cherry tomatoes, halved
- 2 Tbsp. olive oil
- 1 Tbsp. white wine vinegar
- 2 Tbsp. capers
- ¼ Cup of chopped fresh basil
- Grated Parmesan cheese
- 1 Tsp. Italian seasoning
- ½ Lb. dried pasta, cooked

Cooking Instructions:

1. Preheat the Air Fryer to 400°F.
2. Mix together garlic, olive oil, white wine vinegar, cherry tomatoes, shallots, capers, salt, freshly ground black pepper and Italian seasoning in a bowl.
3. Pour the mixture into the Air Fryer basket. Air-fry for 20 minutes. Keep on shaking the basket until cooking time is completed.
4. Pour tomato sauce into the hot pasta, stir in fresh basil, salt and freshly ground black pepper to taste. Make grated Parmesan Cheese available.
5. Serve and enjoy!!!

Messy Sloppy Joes Cheesy Fries

Preparation Time: 15 minutes
Cook Time: 31 minutes
Total Time: 46 minutes
Serves: 2

Ingredients:

- 200g Tinned Tomatoes
- 5 Medium Potatoes
- 1 Tsp. Bolognese Seasoning
- Salt and Pepper
- 28g Cheddar Cheese
- 200g Minced Beef
- 1 Large Onion peeled and diced
- 2 Tbsp. Olive Oil
- 1 Tbsp. Thyme
- 1 Tbsp. Oregano
- 1 Tsp. Basil
- 1 Tbsp. Garlic Puree
- 1 Tbsp. Tomato Puree

Cooking Instructions:

1. Peel and chop off your into small chips. Preheat your Air Fryer to 180°C.
2. Put the potatoes in the Air Fryer and Air-fry for 20 minutes with 1 Tbsp. olive oil. Keep on shaking the basket until cooking time is completed.
3. Air-fry the onions with the remaining olive oil for about 1 minute. Put garlic puree, tomato puree, mix and Air-fry at 180°C for 10 minutes.
4. Put all the seasoning and the tinned tomatoes and stir properly. Flip them onto a serving plate and top with cheddar cheese.
5. Serve and enjoy!!!

Spam Fritters

Preparation Time: 5 minutes
Cook Time: 8 minutes
Total Time: 13 minutes
Serves: 4
Calories: 639 kcal

Ingredients:

- 1 Medium Egg Beaten
- 400g Spam
- 200g Gluten Free Oats
- 28g Cheddar Cheese
- Salt and Pepper
- 100g Plain Flour

Cooking Instructions:

1. In a food blender, blend your gluten free oats.
2. Prepare a production line and put the beaten egg into a mixing bowl while you put plain flour in a separate mixing bowl.
3. Put salt and pepper to the flour and give it a good stir. Stir in grated cheddar cheese to your oats.
4. Slice the spam into sticks and roll them in the flour, dip them in the egg and finally dip them in the oats.
5. Place them in the Air fryer as many as can fit in. Air-fry at 360ºF for 8 minutes.
6. Serve and enjoy!!!

Sweet Potato Burger Buns

Preparation Time: 3 minutes
Cook Time: 10 minutes
Total Time: 13 minutes
Serves: 4
Calories: 50 kcal

Ingredients:

- 4 Medium Paleo Burgers
- Hamburger Press
- 2 Tsp. Olive Oil
- Salt and Pepper
- 1 Large Sweet Potato

Cooking Instructions:

1. Begin by peeling and chopping your sweet potatoes to burger buns shape (2 slices for each burger).
2. Rub the olive oil on the potatoes and season with salt and pepper.
3. Put them in the Air Fryer and Air-fry at 360°F for 10 minutes.
4. Serve and enjoy!!!

Potato Galette

Preparation Time: 10 minutes
Cook Time: 35 minutes
Total Time: 45 minutes
Serves: 3

Ingredients:

- ½ Shallot, minced
- 2 Tbsp. fresh thyme leaves
- 1 Lb. Yukon gold potatoes
- 4 Oz. grated Gruyère cheese
- Sprigs of fresh thyme
- ¼ Cup of butter, melted
- Salt and freshly ground black pepper

Cooking Instructions:

1. Peel, slice your potatoes and put them in a large bowl. Put shallot, fresh thyme, melted butter, salt and pepper. Mix them properly.
2. Keep any long piece of aluminium foil on the counter top. Put the potatoes as many that can enter the foil (the foil should not be longer than the Air Fryer basket).
3. Pour ⅓ of the cheese on the potatoes. Do this again with 2 more layers of potato slices and cheese.
4. Preheat the Air Fryer to 380°F. Put the foil into the Air Fryer basket and loosely folding the fold on the potatoes. Air-fry at 380°F for 30 minutes.
5. Open the Air Fryer; drain out the fat by making some holes in the bottom of the foil. Air-fry for another 5 minutes. Top with sprigs of fresh thyme.
6. Serve and enjoy!!!

Broccoli with Sweet Soy Drizzle

Preparation Time: 10 minutes
Cook Time: 30 minutes
Total Time: 40 minutes
Serves 4

Ingredients:

- 1 Cup of soy sauce
- Olive oil
- 1 Tsp. whole black peppercorns
- 1 Cinnamon stick
- 1 Clove garlic, sliced
- 1 Cup of sugar
- ½ Cup of water
- 2 Green sliced onions
- 1 Head broccoli, broken in florets (4 cups)
- ½-inch Piece of fresh ginger, peeled and sliced

Cooking Instructions:

1. Mix together water and sugar in a medium saucepan and stir properly. Boil the mixture. Reduce the heat and simmer for about 20 minutes.
2. Get the pan out from the heat and put peppercorns, ginger, cinnamon stick, soy sauce, sliced garlic and green onions.
3. Preheat the Air Fryer to 400ºF. Put the broccoli florets in the olive oil. Put salt and freshly ground black pepper.
4. Air-fry at 400ºF for 10 minutes. Keep on shaking the basket until cooking time is completed. Top with the sweet soy sauce.
5. Serve and enjoy!!!

Roasted Vegetable Pasta Salad

Preparation Time: 10 minutes
Cook Time: 15 minutes
Total Time: 25 minutes
Serves 6
Ingredients:
- 1 Cup grape tomatoes, halved
- ½ Cup pitted Kalamata olives, halved
- 1 Large Orange pepper
- ¼ Cup of olive oil
- 2 Tbsp. chopped fresh basil
- 1 Large Green pepper
- 1 Large Red pepper
- 1 Zucchini, sliced in half moons
- 1 Yellow squash, sliced in half moons
- 1 Red onion, sliced
- Salt and fresh ground black pepper
- 1 Lb penne rigate or rigatoni, cooked
- 3 Tbsp. balsamic vinegar
- 4 Oz. brown mushrooms, halved
- 1 Tsp. Italian seasoning

Cooking Instructions:
1. Preheat the Air Fryer to 380°F. In a large mixing bowl, mix together zucchini, mushrooms, yellow squash, peppers and red onion.
2. Sprinkle with olive oil and mix thoroughly. Put the Italian seasoning alongside with salt and pepper. Air-fry for about 15 minutes.
3. Keep on shaking the basket until cooking time is completed. Mix together the roasted vegetables, tomatoes, cooked pasta, balsamic vinegar and olives in a large bowl.
4. Put extra olive oil for proper coating and season with salt and freshly ground black pepper to taste.
5. Put the salad into Refrigerator for about 5 hours. Top with fresh basil.
6. Serve and enjoy!!!

Potato Chips with Sour Cream and Onion Dip

Preparation Time: 10 minutes
Cook Time: 18 minutes
Total Time: 28 minutes
Serves 3
Ingredients:
- Olive oil
- 2 Large potatoes
- Sea salt and freshly ground black pepper

Sour Cream and Onion Dip:
- ¼ Tsp. lemon juice
- 2 Scallions, white part only minced
- ¼ Tsp. salt
- Freshly ground black pepper
- ½ Cup of sour cream
- 1 Tbsp. olive oil

Cooking Instructions:
1. Slice you're your potatoes to $^{1/8}$ inches. Wash them properly and soak them with cold water in a sizeable bowl for about 10 minutes.
2. Drain and dry the potato slices using a clean kitchen towel. Preheat the Air Fryer to 300°F. Spray oil on the potato chips.
3. Divide the potatoes and Air-fry in two batches at 300°F for about 18 minutes. Keep on shaking the basket until cooking time is completed.
4. Season the finished chips with sea salt and freshly ground black pepper. For the sour cream and onion dip, mix together the olive oil, sour cream, scallions, lemon juice, salt and pepper.
5. Serve and enjoy!!!

Thyme Garlic Tomatoes

Preparation Time: 8 minutes
Cook Time: 15 minutes
Total Time: 23 minutes
Serves 4

Ingredients:

- 1 Clove garlic, minced
- ½ Tsp. dried thyme
- 4 Roma tomatoes
- Salt and freshly ground black pepper
- 1 Tbsp. olive oil

Cooking Instructions:

1. Preheat the Air Fryer to 390° F.
2. Shred the tomatoes in half and get the seeds out. Mix the tomatoes with the olive oil, garlic, salt, pepper, and thyme in a bowl.
3. Place the shredded side of the tomatoes up in the Air Fryer and Air-fry at 390ºF for 15 minutes. Remove them onto plates.
4. Serve and enjoy!!!

Brussel Sprouts with Bacon

Preparation Time: 3 minutes
Cook Time: 15 minutes
Total Time: 18 minutes
Serves 2
Calories: 187 kcal

Ingredients:

- 450g Brussel Sprouts
- Salt Pepper
- 4 Slices Back Bacon

Cooking Instructions:

1. Prepare the Brussel by removing the core and the outside skin of the Brussel Sprouts and put them into your Air Fryer.
2. Air-fry at 360°F at 10 minutes. Mince your bacon. Trim out the fat and put them into Air Fryer.
3. Serve and enjoy!!!

Pepperoni and Cheese Pizza Chips

Preparation Time: 3 minutes
Cook Time: 15 minutes
Total Time: 18 minutes
Serves 2
Calories: 329 kcal
Ingredients:
- 28g Diced Tomatoes
- 4 Tsp. Olive Oil
- 1 Tbsp. Oregano
- 2 Large Potatoes
- 15g Pepperoni
- 40g Hard Cheese
- Salt and Pepper

Cooking Instructions:
1. Peel and cut your potatoes into frying sizes.
2. Put them into the Air Fryer with olive oil and Air-fry at 360ºF for 12 minutes.
3. Remove the Chips from the Air Fryer and lay them on the Air Fryer Baking Pan.
4. Mix together the oregano, freshly diced tomatoes, salt and pepper. Spread them on the chips. Pour in cheese and pepperoni.
5. Air-fry at 320ºF 3 minutes. Flip them onto a serving plate.
6. Serve and enjoy!!!

AIR FRYER VEGAN & VEGETARIAN RECIPES

Potato Wedges

Preparation Time: 2 minutes
Cook Time: 25 minutes
Total Time: 27 minutes
Serves: 4
Calories: 159 kcal

Ingredients:
- 4 Large Potatoes
- Salt and Pepper
- 1 Tbsp. Olive Oil
- 1 Tbsp. Cajun Spice

Cooking Instructions:
1. Peel and slice your potatoes into wedge shapes and put them in your Air Fryer.
2. Pour 1 Tbsp. olive oil Air-fry at 190ºC for 25 minutes. Keep on shaking the basket until cooking time is completed.
3. Flip them onto a serving plate, season with salt, pepper and Cajun spice.
4. Serve and enjoy!!!

Curly Fries

Preparation Time: 5 minutes
Cook Time: 15 minutes
Total Time: 20 minutes
Serves: 4

Ingredients:

- 2 Tbsp. Coconut Oil
- 2 Large Potatoes
- 2 Tbsp. Olive Oil
- 1 Tbsp. Homemade Tomato Ketchup
- Salt and Pepper

Cooking Instructions:

1. Peel and chop your potatoes into the shape of curly fries.
2. Mix together the coconut oil, olive oil and potatoes in a small mixing bowl.
3. Put them in the Air Fryer and Air-fry at 180ºC for 15 minutes. Season with salt and pepper. Top with homemade tomato ketchup.
4. Serve and enjoy!!!

Coconut Oil Latte Overnight Oats with Greek Yogurt

Preparation Time: 5 minutes
Total Time: 5 minutes
Serves: 1
Calories 217 kcal
Ingredients:
- ⅓ Cup of Non-fat vanilla Greek yogurt
- ½ Tsp. Vanilla extract
- Sweetener of choice
- ½ Cup of Rolled, old fashioned oat
- ½ Cup of Strong brewed coffee

Cooking Instructions:
1. In a medium mixing bowl, mix together all ingredients and add sweetening to your taste.
2. Refrigerate for at least 6 hours.
3. Serve and enjoy!!!

Smoothie with Almond Milk

Preparation Time: 5 minutes
Total Time: 5 minutes
Serves: 1
Calories 332 kcal
Ingredients:
- 1 Cup of Unsweetened almond milk
- 1 Cup of Crushed ice
- ¼ Cup of Avocado
- 3 Tbsp. Monk fruit
- 2 Tbsp. Natural creamy peanut butter
- 1 Tbsp. Unsweetened cocoa powder

Cooking Instructions:
1. Gather all ingredients and put them into a food blender and smoothly blend them.
2. Serve and enjoy!!!

Sparkling Holiday Champagne Sangria

Preparation Time: 5 minutes
Total Time: 5 minutes
Serves: 8
Calories 183 kcal

Ingredients:

- 4 Orange, sliced
- 1 750ml Bottle Brut Champagne
- 3 Cups of 100% Cranberry juice
- 2 Cups of Fresh cranberries

Cooking Instructions:

1. In a medium bowl, mix together all the ingredients except the champagne in a large pitcher.
2. Refrigerate at least 5 hours. Stir in champagne.
3. Serve and enjoy!!!

Ginger Snap Cookie Steamer Drink

Preparation Time: 5 minutes
Total Time: 5 minutes
Serves: 2
Calories 225 kcal

Ingredients:

- 2 Cups of Light Coconut Milk
- ¼ Tsp. Ground ginger
- Coconut Whipped cream
- 2 Tbsp. Coconut sugar or brown sugar
- 1 Tsp. Cinnamon
- ¼ Tsp. Ground cloves
- 1 Tbsp. Molasses

Cooking Instructions:

1. In a medium bowl, mix together all the ingredients and warm them on low heat for few minutes.
2. Share them into 2 cups and top coconut whipped cream.
3. Serve and enjoy!!!

Vegetable Fries

Preparation Time: 5 minutes
Cook Time: 15 minutes
Total Time: 20 minutes
Serves: 4
Calories: 116 kcal

Ingredients:

- 150g Sweet Potato
- Pinch Basil
- Salt and Pepper
- 150g Courgette
- 2 Tbsp. Olive Oil
- 1 Tsp. Thyme
- Pinch Mixed Spice
- 150g Carrots

Cooking Instructions:

1. Peel your potatoes and carrots.
2. Slice your potatoes, carrots and courgettes into the shape of chunky chips.
3. Put the chips in the Air Fryer, put olive oil and Air-fry at 180ºC for 18 minutes.
4. Keep on shaking the basket until cooking time is completed.
5. Flip them onto a bowl and put seasoning.
6. Serve and enjoy!!!

Meatless Monday Macaroni and Cheese Toasties

Preparation Time: 3 minutes
Cook Time: 10 minutes
Total Time: 13 minutes
Serves: 1
Calories: 493 kcal

Ingredients:
- 25g Cheddar Cheese
- Salt and Pepper
- 2 Slices White Bread
- 4 Tbsp. Macaroni Cheese
- 1 Small Egg beaten

Cooking Instructions:
1. Spread macaroni cheese and cheddar cheese on the bread.

2. Keep the other slice of bread on top and cut it slanting and rub egg on outside of your bread. Put salt and pepper.

3. Put them into the Air Fryer and Air-fry at180°C at 5 minutes.

4. Serve and enjoy!!!

Five Cheese Pull apart Bread

Preparation Time: 15 minutes
Cook Time: 6 minutes
Total Time: 21 minutes
Serves: 2
Calories: 653 kcal

Ingredients:

- 30g Edam Cheese
- 2 Tsp. Chives
- 1 Large Bread Loaf
- 100g Butter
- 30g Goats Cheese
- 30g Mozzarella Cheese
- 30g Soft Cheese
- Salt and Pepper
- 2 Tsp. Garlic Puree
- 30g Cheddar Cheese

Cooking Instructions:

1. Slice your hard cheese into four piles and set aside.
2. Using medium heat, melt the butter in a saucepan and put chives, garlic, salt and pepper and then Air-fry for about 2 minutes and mix them properly.
3. Make a small slits in your bread. Put garlic butter in each of the little slit wholes. Pour in soft cheese.
4. In any place you did not make a slit spread small cheddar and goat cheese while you put Edam and mozzarella to those that have not been filled.
5. Put in the Air Fryer and Air-fry for 4 minutes.
6. Serve and enjoy!!!

Sticky Pumpkin Wedges

Preparation Time: 5 minutes
Cook Time: 25 minutes
Total Time: 30 minutes
Serves: 2

Ingredients:

- 1 Tsp. Turmeric
- Salt and Pepper
- ½ Medium Pumpkin
- 1 Tbsp. Balsamic Vinegar
- 1 Tbsp. Paprika
- 1 Lime juice

Cooking Instructions:

1. Cut half of your pumpkin into medium sized wedges and put them into your Air Fryer grilling pan.
2. Air-fry at 180°C for 20 minutes. Season with half of your seasonings, vinegar and lime.
3. Flip them over; put the remaining ingredients and then Air-fry at 200°C.
4. Serve and enjoy!!!

Veggie Pakoras

Preparation Time: 20 minutes
Cook Time: 20 minutes
Total Time: 40 minutes
Serves: 2

Ingredients:

- 1 Large Sweet Potato
- Salt and Pepper
- 3 Oz Indian Granola
- Left-over Vegetables

Cooking Instructions:

1. Peel, slice and put your potatoes Air Fryer basket and Air-fry for 15 minutes.
2. Pour it to the leftover vegetables and mash properly.
3. Blend the Indian granola in a food blender. Put salt and pepper and mix properly. Keep the vegetables into pakora shapes with your hands.
4. Dip the vegetables in the granola mixture. Keep them on a baking pan and Air-fry at 180°C for 20 minutes.
5. Serve and enjoy!!!

AIR FRYER BURGER RECIPES

Herb and Cheese-Stuffed Burgers

Preparation Time: 20 minutes
Cook Time: 20 minutes
Total Time: 40 minutes
Serves: 4

Ingredients:
- 1 Lb. lean ground beef
- 4 Hamburger buns, split
- 2 Tbsp. minced fresh parsley
- 3 Tsp. Dijon mustard, divided
- 3 Tbsp. dry bread crumbs
- 2 Tbsp. ketchup
- ½ Tsp. salt
- ½ Tsp. dried rosemary, crushed
- ¼ Cup of cubed cheddar cheese
- 2 Green onions, thinly sliced
- ¼ Tsp. dried sage leaves
- lettuce leaves and tomato slices (optional)

Cooking Instructions:
1. Preheat your Air Fryer to 375°F.
2. Mix together green onions, parsley teaspoon mustard and cheddar cheese in a small mixing bowl.
3. In a different bowl, mix together ketchup, seasonings, crumbs and remaining mustard. Put beef into bread crumb mix properly.
4. Cut the mixture into 8 patties. Spread cheese mixture on the top. Close the edges.
5. Put the burgers in the Air Fryer and Air-fry for about 7 minutes.
6. Serve and enjoy!!!

Hamburgers

Preparation Time: 3 minutes
Cook Time: 17 minutes
Total Time: 20 minutes
Serves: 2

Ingredients:

- 2 Whole Wheat Dinner Rolls
- 320g Mixed Mince
- 1 Tsp Mustard
- 2 Medium Potatoes
- 2 Slices Mozzarella Cheese
- ¼ Small Onion
- 2 Tsp. Mixed Herbs
- Salt and Pepper
- ½ Tsp. Olive Oil

Cooking Instructions:

1. Peel and slice your potatoes into the shape of French Fries with ½ Tsp. olive oil.
2. Slice and mince your onions and mix them in a bowl with the seasoning. Cut the prepared mixture into hamburger patty shapes.
3. Put them on one side into the Air Fryer while you keep the other French Fries on the other side.
4. Air-fry at 180ºC for 15 minutes. On the top of both burgers, put one slice of mozzarella cheese and Air-fry for another 2 minutes at 160ºC.
5. Serve and enjoy!!!

Lamb Burgers

Preparation Time: 3 minutes
Cook Time: 18 minutes
Total Time: 21 minutes
Serves: 4
Calories: 478 kcal
Ingredients:
Lamb Burger:
- 650g Minced Lamb
- 1 Tbsp. Moroccan Spice
- Salt and Pepper
- 2 Tsp. Garlic Puree
- 1 Tsp. Harissa Paste

Greek Dip:
- 3 Tbsp. Greek Yoghurt
- ½ Tsp. Oregano
- 1 Small Lemon juice
- 1 Tsp. Moroccan Spice

Cooking Instructions:
1. Mix your lamb burger ingredients in a small mixing bowl and make them into lamb burger shapes.
2. Put the burgers in the Air Fryer and Air-fry at 360ºF for 18 minutes.
3. For grip dip, mix all the ingredients together.
4. Serve and enjoy!!!

Leftover Turkey Burgers

Preparation Time: 2 minutes
Cook Time: 20 minutes
Total Time: 22 minutes
Serves: 12
Calories: 114 kcal

Ingredients:

- 100g Gluten Free Oats
- 500g Roast Dinner Leftovers
- 100g Cheddar Cheese

Cooking Instructions:

1. Preheat your Air Fryer to 180°C.
2. In a mixing bowl, mix the leftovers with cheese and oats.
3. Put 4 at a time in the Air Fryer at 180°C for 20 minutes.
4. Top with burger bun or fried eggs.
5. Serve and enjoy!!!

Mediterranean Paleo Burgers

Preparation Time: 3 minutes
Cook Time: 15 minutes
Total Time: 18 minutes
Serves: 2
Calories: 585 kcal

Ingredients:
- Sweet Potato Fries
- ¼ Small Onion
- ½ Tsp. Rosemary
- Salt and Pepper
- 2 Tbsp. Fried Onions
- 2 Fried Eggs
- 1 Tsp. Garlic Puree
- 350g Mixed Mince
- 2 Tsp. Oregano
- 1 Tsp. Thyme
- 1 Tsp. Parsley

Cooking Instructions:
1. Mince ¼ of an onion.
2. Put the garlic, onion and mixed mince with the seasoning in a mixing bowl. Prepare them into hamburger shapes.
3. Put them in the Air Fryer and Air-fry at 360°F for 15 minutes. Top with fried onions and eggs.
4. Serve and enjoy!!!

Gourmet Blue Cheese Burgers

Preparation Time: 5 minutes
Cook Time: 6 minutes
Total Time: 11 minutes
Serves: 4

Ingredients:

- 3 Lbs. lean ground meat
- 4 Oz. blue cheese
- 1 Tsp. dry mustard
- 12 Brioche hamburger rolls
- 1/8 Cup of minced fresh chives
- 1 Tsp. Worcestershire sauce
- 1 Tsp. black pepper
- 1 Tsp. salt
- ¼ Tsp. hot pepper sauce

Optional Toppings: Lettuce, red onions and tomato slices.

Cooking Instructions:

1. Mix together the blue cheese, chives, meat, hot pepper sauce, salt, pepper, dry mustard and Worcestershire sauce in a mixing bowl.
2. Put the bowl in the refrigerator for about an hour.
3. Make them into patties shape and lay them in the Air Fryer basket. Air-fry at 360°F. Flip them over and cook again.
4. Serve and enjoy!!!

Nandos Beanie Burger

Preparation Time: 5 minutes
Cook Time: 12 minutes
Total Time: 17 minutes
Serves: 4

Ingredients:
- 1 Tbsp. Homemade Nandos Marinade
- 6 Bread Buns
- Salad Garnish
- 2 Cans Black Beans
- 8 Medium Slices Whole-meal Bread
- 3 Garlic Cloves
- 1 Lime juice and rind
- 1 Tbsp. Paprika
- 1 Tbsp. Cumin
- Salt and Pepper
- ½ Onion
- 1 Red Onion

Cooking Instructions:
1. Wash the black beans. Sieve out and remove any water in it. Blend the sliced bread in a food blender.
2. Mince your onions and garlic. Mix the blended bread, all the seasoning, onions, black beans, garlic, lime and marinade in a mixing bowl.
3. Make into 6 burgers shape and put them in the refrigerator one hour.
4. Put them in the Air Fryer and Air-fry at 347ºF for 12 minutes. Top with salad garnish.
5. Serve and enjoy!!!

Quinoa Burgers

Preparation Time: 7 minutes
Cook Time: 17 minutes
Total Time: 24 minutes
Serves: 4

Ingredients:

- 1 Cup Cooked Quinoa
- Salt
- 2 Small Garlic Cloves, minced
- ½ Cup of Boiled Potatoes, mashed
- Oil
- 1 Tsp Garam Masala Spice Powder
- ½ Medium Onion, chopped finely
- ½ Cup of Red Capsicum, diced
- ¾ Cup of Leftover Cooked Rice
- ½ Cup of Chickpea Flour

Cooking Instructions:

1. Put all the ingredients into a small mixing bowl and mix properly.
2. Make them into burgers shape. Keep aside.
3. Put them into the Air Fryer and Air-fry at180ºC for 17 minutes.
4. Serve and enjoy!!!

Simple Black Bean Burger

Preparation Time: 10 minutes
Cook Time: 25 minutes
Total Time: 35 minutes
Serves: 6

Ingredients:

- 1 1/3 Cups of rolled oats
- ¼ Tsp. chipotle Chile powder
- ½ Tsp. garlic powder
- 16 Oz. black beans
- 1 Tsp. soy sauce
- 1 ¼ Tsp. mild chili powder
- 3/4 Cup of salsa
- ½ Cup of corn kernels (optional)

Cooking Instructions:

1. Put the oats into a food blender with an S-blade and chop them. Pour in all ingredients except the corn and blend them.
2. Put corn into a mixing bowl, pour in the blended mixture and keep them in the refrigerator for about 15 minutes.
3. Preheat the Air Fryer to 375ºF. Put the burgers in the Air Fry and Air-fry for 15 minutes.
4. Serve and enjoy!!!

KFC Zinger Chicken Burger

Preparation Time: 10 minutes
Cook Time: 15 minutes
Total Time: 25 minutes
Serves: 4
Calories: 549 kcal

Ingredients:

- 6 Chicken Breasts
- 1 Tsp. Paprika
- Salt and Pepper
- 10ml KFC Spice Blend
- 100ml Bread Crumbs
- 1 Tsp. Worcester Sauce
- 1 Tsp. Mustard Powder
- 1 Small Egg beaten
- 50g Plain Flour

Cooking Instructions:

1. In a food blender, mince your chicken and put mustard, paprika, Worcester sauce, salt and pepper.
2. Shred your chicken into burger shapes and set aside. Place your egg in a bowl.
3. Put flour in another mixing bowl and then KFC spice blend mix with your bread crumbs.
4. Roll your Zinger burgers in the flour, the egg and then the bread crumbs.
5. Put them into the Air Fryer and Air-fry at 180°C for 15 minutes.
6. Serve and enjoy!!!

Chicken Avocado Burgers

Preparation Time: 2 minutes
Cook Time: 12 minutes
Total Time: 14 minutes
Serves: 2
Calories: 707 kcal

Ingredients:

* 400g Avocado
* 400g Minced Chicken
* 1 Tbsp. Mexican Seasoning

Cooking Instructions:

1. Wash, peel and slice your avocado.
2. Chop only 3 of the avocado slices into small cubes and keep the rest like that.
3. Mix together minced chicken, chunks of avocado and Mexican seasoning in a mixing bowl.
4. Cut them into the shape of chicken burger patty. Put them in the Air Fryer and Air-fry at 360°F for 12 minutes.
5. Serve and enjoy!!!

AIR FRYER APPETIZER RECIPES

Party Meatballs

Preparation Time: 20 minutes
Cook Time: 15 minutes
Total Time: 35 minutes
Serves: 24
Calories: 83 kcal

Ingredients:

- 1 Lb Mince Beef
- ½ Tsp. Dry Mustard
- 3 Gingersnaps crushed
- ¾ Cup of Tomato Ketchup
- 1 Tbsp. Tabasco
- 1 Tbsp. Lemon Juice
- ½ Cup of Brown Sugar
- 2 ½ Tbsp. Worcester Sauce
- ¼ Cup of Vinegar

Cooking Instructions:

1. Mix together all the seasoning including mince beef properly in a large mixing bowl.
2. Make them into meatballs shape and put them in the Air Fryer. Air-fry at 190°C. Put them on sticks.
3. Serve and enjoy!!!

Honey Lime Chicken Wings

Preparation Time: 5 minutes
Cook Time: 15 minutes
Total Time: 11 minutes
Serves: 4

Ingredients:

- ½ Crush black pepper
- 2 Tbsp. lime juice
- 16 Mid joint chicken wings
- ½ Tsp. sea salt
- ¼ Tsp. white pepper powder
- 2 Tbsp. light soya sauce
- 2 Tbsp. good quality honey

Cooking Instructions:

1. Wash the mid wings clean and dry them using kitchen towel.
2. Pour all marinates into a glass dish. Toss in mid wings, mix properly and put them in the refrigerator for about 6 hours.
3. Remove them and put in the Air Fryer. Air-fry at 180°C for 6 minutes. Turn them over and Air-fry at 180°C for 6 minutes.
4. Turn them over for the last time and Air-fry at 200°C for 3 minutes.
5. Serve and enjoy!!!

Parmesan Dill Fried Pickle Chips

Preparation Time: 14 minutes
Cook Time: 20 minutes
Total Time: 34 minutes
Serves: 4

Ingredients:

- 2 Eggs
- ¼ Tsp. dried dill weed
- 2/3 Cup of panko bread crumbs
- 1/3 Cup of grated Parmesan
- 32 Oz. jar whole large dill pickles

Cooking Instructions:

1. Cut the pickles slantingly into ¼ inch thickness, keep them inside layers of paper towels and pat dry.
2. Break the eggs into a bowl and set aside. Put Parmesan, dill weed and Panko bread crumbs in a bag that can be sealed and shake to mix properly.
3. Using about 4 pieces at a time, bury the pickle slices in the egg mixture and finally in panko mixture.
4. Place the chips in the Air Fryer about half of the chips and Air-fry at 397ºF for 10 minutes. Do this for the remaining chips.
5. Serve and enjoy!!!

Mozzarella Sticks

Preparation Time: 10 minutes
Cook Time: 12 minutes
Total Time: 22 minutes
Serves: 4

Ingredients:

- 2 Eggs
- 1 Cup of bread crumbs
- 3 Tbsp. Milk
- 1 Lb. Mozzarella cheese
- ½ Cup of Flour

Cooking Instructions:

1. Slice the Mozzarella cheese into the size of 3 x ½ inch sticks.
2. Put flour and bread crumbs in two different bowls. Whisk together milk and eggs in another bowl.
3. Bury the cheese sticks into egg mixture, flour and bread crumbs. Place the cheese sticks on a pan and put them in refrigerator for about 2 hours.
4. Put sizeable number of the sticks into Air Fryer basket and Air-fry at 400°F for 12 minutes.
5. Serve and enjoy!!!

Cheese Toastie

Preparation Time: 1 minute
Cook Time: 8 minutes
Total Time: 9 minutes
Serves: 4
Calories: 302 kcal

Ingredients:
- 8 Slices Whole-meal Bread
- 150g Cheddar Cheese

Cooking Instructions:
1. Prepare the cheese and bread into cheese sandwiches.
2. Put in the Air Fryer and Air-fry at 180ºC for 4 minutes. (2 at a time).
3. Serve and enjoy!!!

Buttermilk Fried Chicken

Preparation Time: 10 minutes
Cook Time: 16 minutes
Total Time: 26 minutes
Serves: 4
Ingredients:
Buttermilk Marinade:
- 2 Tsp. black pepper
- 1 Tsp. paprika
- 2 Cups of buttermilk
- 2 Tsp. salt

Flour Mixture:
- 2 Cups of flour
- 4 Boneless Chicken Breasts
- 1 Tbsp. of baking powder
- 1 Tbsp. of garlic powder

Cooking Instructions:
1. Mix separately the flour and buttermilk ingredients.
2. Preheat Air Fryer at 360°F. Bury your chicken into the buttermilk mixture and then roll it in the flour mixture.
3. Place them in the Air Fryer basket. Air-fry at 180°C for 8 minutes. Turn them over and cook for further 8 minutes.
4. Serve and enjoy!!!

Spicy Dill Pickle Fries

Preparation Time: 15 minutes
Cook Time: 15 minutes
Total Time: 30 minutes
Serves: 4

Ingredients:

- ¼ Cup of milk
- 1 Egg, beaten
- 1 ½ jars spicy dill pickle spears (16 Oz.)
- 1 Cup all-purpose flour
- Cooking spray
- ½ Tsp. paprika
- 1 Cup of panko bread crumbs

Cooking Instructions:

1. Wash your pickles and dry them. Put paprika and flour in a small mixing bowl and mix properly.
2. Put milk and beaten egg in a separate mixing bowl while you put panko in another mixing bowl.
3. Preheat your Air Fryer to 400ºF. Bury the pickles in the flour, egg and bread crumbs mixtures respectively.
4. Put on a plate and spray with cooking spray. Set aside. Keep the pickles into the Air Fryer basket and Air-fry for 14 minutes.
5. Keep on shaking the basket until cooking time is completed.
6. Serve and enjoy!!!

Zucchini Gratin

Preparation Time: 10 minutes
Cook Time: 15 minutes
Total Time: 25 minutes
Serves: 3

Ingredients:

- 4 Tbsp. grated Parmesan cheese
- 1 Tbsp. vegetable oil
- 2 Zucchini
- 1 Tbsp. chopped fresh parsley
- 2 Tbsp. bread crumbs
- Pepper
- Salt

Cooking Instructions:

1. Preheat your Air Fryer to 180ºC.
2. Cut zucchini into 2 and cut the half again into another halves. Put them into the Air Fryer.
3. Mix together the parsley, cheese, oil, bread crumbs, and freshly ground black pepper to taste.
4. Pour zucchini with the prepared parsley mixture and put them into Air Fryer basket.
5. Air-fry in two batches at 180ºC for 15 minutes.
6. Serve and enjoy!!!

Crinkle Cut Chips

Preparation Time: 2 minutes
Cook Time: 15 minutes
Total Time: 17 minutes
Serves: 4

Ingredients:

- 1 Large Potato
- 1 Tbsp. Olive Oil
- Salt and Pepper

Cooking Instructions:

1. Peel and slice your potato into crinkle size chips and then put salt and pepper on the chips.
2. Pour olive oil on the chips; put them into the Air Fryer and Air-fry for at 400ºF. Keep on shaking the basket until cooking time is completed.
3. Serve and enjoy!!!

Buffalo-Ranch Chickpeas

Preparation Time: 5 minutes
Cook Time: 20 minutes
Total Time: 25 minutes
Serves: 4

Ingredients:

- 1 (15 Oz.) can chickpeas, drained and rinsed
- 1 Tbsp. dry ranch dressing mix
- 2 Tbsp. Buffalo wing sauce

Cooking Instructions:

1. Preheat your Air Fryer to 350°F.
2. Keep some paper towels on a baking pan and place the chickpeas on it. Put one layer of paper towel and press down so some unwanted liquid can be removed.
3. Put the chickpeas into a mixing bowl, put ranch dressing and wing sauce into the bowl and mix properly.
4. Put the mixed chickpeas into the Air Fryer basket and Air-fry at 320°F for 8 minutes.
5. After the cooking time is up, shake and Air-fry for 2 times at 5 minutes intervals. Shake and Air-fry finally for 2 minutes.
6. Serve and enjoy!!!

Sweet Potato Fries

Preparation Time: 5 minutes
Cook Time: 15 minutes
Total Time: 20 minutes
Serves: 2
Calories: 319 kcal

Ingredients:

- 300g Sweet Potatoes
- 3 Tbsp. Olive Oil
- Salt and Pepper
- 1 Tsp. Mustard Powder

Cooking Instructions:

1. Peel and slice your potatoes into chunky chips.
2. Put enough olive oil into the Air Fryer and pour in the chips.
3. Air-fry at 180°C for 15 minutes. Keep on shaking the basket until cooking time is completed.
4. Put the potatoes in a bowl when they are done. Put 1 Tbsp. olive oil and seasoning. Mix properly.
5. Serve and enjoy!!!

AIR FRYER DESSERT RECIPES

Chocolate Mug Cake

Preparation Time: 2 minutes
Cook Time: 10 minutes
Total Time: 12 minutes
Serves: 1
Calories: 501 kcal

Ingredients:
- ¼ Cup Self Raising Flour
- 5 Tbsp. Caster Sugar
- 1 Tbsp. Cocoa Powder
- 3 Tbsp. Whole Milk
- 3 Tsp. Coconut Oil

Cooking Instructions:
1. In a mug, combine all the ingredients together. Mix thoroughly.
2. Put the mug into the Air Fryer and Air-fry at 200ºC for 10 minutes.
3. Rinse and repeat for the other mugs to have chocolate hit.
4. Serve and enjoy!!!

Fruit Crumble Mug Cakes

Preparation Time: 15 minutes
Cook Time: 15 minutes
Total Time: 30 minutes
Serves: 4
Calories: 380 kcal

Ingredients:

- 30g Gluten Free Oats
- 110g Plain Flour
- 25g Brown Sugar
- 4 Plums
- Handful Blueberries
- 1 Tbsp. Honey
- 1 Small Apple
- 50g Butter
- 30g Caster Sugar
- 1 Small Pear
- 1 Small Peach

Cooking Instructions:

1. Preheat the Air Fryer to 160°C.
2. Make use of the corer, remove the stones and the cores from the fruit and mince them into small square pieces.
3. Put the fruit in the mugs and spray brown sugar and honey to cover all the fruit. Keep aside.
4. In a small mixing bowl, mix together the butter, flour and caster sugar. Rub the fat in the mixture, put oats and mix thoroughly.
5. Pour a layer of your crumble on top of the mugs. Put them into the Air Fryer.
6. Air-fry at 160°C for 10 minutes at 160c. Shake the basket and Air-fry for another 5 minutes at 200°C.
7. Serve and enjoy!!!

Frugal Pineapple Cake

Preparation Time: 10 minutes
Cook Time: 40 minutes
Total Time: 50 minutes
Serves: 4
Calories: 612 kcal

Ingredients:

- 1 Medium Eggs
- 2 Tbsp. Whole Milk
- 225g Self Raising Flour
- 100g Butter
- 100ml Pineapple Juice
- 50g Dark Chocolate grated
- 100g Caster Sugar
- 200g Pineapple chopped into chunks

Cooking Instructions:

1. Preheat the Air Fryer to 200ºC. Pour oil into your baking pan.
2. In a bowl mix together the butter and the flour. Mix properly.
3. Sprinkle the sugar, dark chocolate, pineapple chunks and juice. Set aside.
4. Whisk the milk and egg in a jug. Combine the liquid mixture with the butter mixture.
5. Place them in the Air Fryer and Air-fry at 200ºC for 40 minutes.
6. Serve and enjoy!!!

White Chocolate Chip Cookies

Preparation Time: 18 minutes
Cook Time: 8 minutes
Total Time: 26 minutes
Serves: 8
Calories: 258 kcal

Ingredients:

- 30ml Honey
- 30ml Whole Milk
- 175g Self Raising Flour
- 75g Brown Sugar
- 60g White Chocolate
- 100g Butter

Cooking Instructions:

1. Make the butter to become soft.
2. Put sugar into the butter and mix thoroughly.
3. Put flour, white chocolate, honey and milk. Mix properly.
4. Prepare the mixture to look like cookie shapes.
5. Put them in the Air Fryer and Air-fry at 180°C for 18 minutes.
6. Serve and enjoy!!!

Banana Bread

Preparation Time: 10 minutes
Cook Time: 25 minutes
Total Time: 35 minutes
Serves: 1 loaf of bread
Calories: 3207 kcal

Ingredients:

- 225g Self Raising Flour
- ¼ Tsp Bicarbonate Of Soda
- 75g Butter
- 175g Caster Sugar
- 2 Medium Eggs
- 450g Bananas weight with peeling
- 100g Chopped Walnuts

Cooking Instructions:

1. Preheat the Air Fryer to 180ºC. Put oil into your baking pan.
2. Mix the flour together with the bicarbonate of soda in a mixing bowl.
3. Cream the sugar and butter in another mixing bowl and put the eggs along with the flour and walnuts.
4. Peel and mash the bananas. Put them to your mixture. Place the mixture in the Air Fryer baking pan and Air-fry at 180ºC for 10 minutes.
5. Shake the basket and Air-fry for another 15 minutes at 170ºC.
6. Serve and enjoy!!!

Mini Apple Pie

Preparation Time: 5 minutes
Cook Time: 18 minutes
Total Time: 23 minutes
Serves: 9
Calories: 84 kcal

Ingredients:

- 75g Plain Flour
- 33g Butter
- 2 Medium Red Apples
- A Pinch of Cinnamon
- 15g Caster Sugar
- Water
- A Pinch of Caster Sugar

Cooking Instructions:

1. Preheat your Air Fryer to 180°C. In a small mixing bowl, put the butter and plain flour.
2. Put the fat into the flour and add sugar. Give it a good mixing and add water that will make the dough to mix properly.
3. Put butter to help stop it sticking and then roll out the pastry and fill your pastry tins.
4. Peel and mince your apples, put them in the tins and spray in sugar and cinnamon.
5. Put an extra pastry layer on the top and make some fork markings. Place them in the Air Fryer and Air-fry at 180°C for 18 minutes.
6. Serve and enjoy!!!

British Lemon Tarts in the Air Fryer

Preparation Time: 15 minutes
Cook Time: 15 minutes
Total Time: 30 minutes
Serves: 8
Calories: 218 kcal
Ingredients:
- 100g Butter
- 225g Plain Flour
- 30g Caster Sugar
- 1 Large Lemon zest and juice
- 4 Tsp. Mrs. Darlington's Lemon Curd
- Pinch of Nutmeg

Cooking Instructions:
1. Mix together the butter, flour and sugar in a large mixing bowl.
2. Mix thoroughly until it looks like breadcrumbs. Put the lemon rind and juice, nutmeg. Put water and mix thoroughly.
3. Roll the pastry with a little flour. Use a little pastry case rub a little flour around them to stop them sticking and then add your pastry.
4. Make your pastry too be thin. Put ½ Tsp. into each of your mini tart containers and then Air-fry at 180ºC for 15 minutes.
5. Serve and enjoy!!!

Apple Dumplings

Preparation Time: 25 minutes
Cook Time: 25 minutes
Total Time: 50 minutes
Serves: 2

Ingredients:
- 2 Small apples
- 2 Tbsp. raisins
- 1 Tbsp. brown sugar
- 2 Sheets puff pastry
- 2 Tbsp. melted butter

Cooking Instructions:
1. Preheat your Air Fryer to 356°F. Peel the apples.
2. Mix together the brown sugar and raisins in a mixing bowl.
3. Put each apple on 1 of the puff pastry pans and then fill the core with the sugar mixture.
4. Fold the pastry around the apple. Keep the apple on a small sheet of foil.
5. This will help to prevent juice from dropping into the Air Fryer. Rub melted butter on the dough.
6. Put them into the Air Fryer and Air-fry at 340°F for 25 minutes.
7. Serve and enjoy!!!

Potato Skins

Preparation Time: 10 minutes
Cook Time: 7 minutes
Total Time: 17 minutes
Serves: 3

Ingredients:

- 10 Small baking potatoes
- Thinly sliced chives.
- Dean's Bacon Cheddar Dip
- ½ Cup of shredded cheddar cheese
- ½ Cup of crumbled bacon

Cooking Instructions

1. Preheat your Air Fryer to 350°F.
2. Put your potatoes into the Air Fryer and bake with oil and spices of your choice.
3. When they are fully baked, slice each of the potatoes into half. Remove some part of the flesh from the inside of the potato.
4. Spray bacon crumbles and cheddar cheese on each half. Put them into the Air Fryer and Air-fry at 350°F for 7 minutes.
5. Flip them onto a serving plate and top with creamy Dean's Dip.
6. Serve and enjoy!!!

Garlic Mashed Potatoes

Preparation Time: 10 minutes
Cook Time: 45 minutes
Total Time: 55 minutes
Serves: 4

Ingredients:

- 5 Lbs. unpeeled red potatoes
- 1 Stick (8 Tbsp.) butter
- 2 Tsp. salt
- 1 Tsp. dried oregano
- 1/2 Cup of grated romano cheese
- 3 Tbsp. chopped garlic

Cooking Instructions:

1. Put salt into a large pot and boil.
2. Put the potatoes into the Air Fryer and Air-fry for 45 minutes.
3. Drain the water out and put cheese, garlic, butter, salt and oregano. Mash the potatoes with any available masher.
4. Serve and enjoy!!!

Mini Cherry and Cheese Streusel Tartlets

Preparation Time: 10 minutes
Cook Time: 19 minutes
Total Time: 29 minutes
Serves: 6

Ingredients:

- 1 Egg
- 6 Oz. cream cheese
- 3 Tbsp. sugar
- 2 Cups of cherry pie filling
- 1 Tbsp. all-purpose flour
- ½ Tsp. vanilla extract
- 6 Packaged mini graham cracker tartlet crusts

Streusel Topping:

- ⅓ Cup of walnuts, chopped
- 3 Tbsp. melted butter
- 5 Tbsp. all-purpose flour
- 2 Tbsp. sugar
- ½ Tsp. ground cinnamon

Cooking Instructions:

1. Preheat your Air Fryer to 330°F.
2. Mix together the sugar, egg, cream cheese, flour and vanilla extract in a small mixing bowl. Put the mixture into tartlets shells.
3. Put three at a time into the Air Fryer and Air-fry at 330°F for 4 minutes. Prepare the streusel topping in a different bowl.
4. Do this by mixing together the flour, walnuts, cinnamon, sugar and melted butter. Mix thoroughly and keep aside.
5. Put 2 Tbsp. of the cherry pie filling into each tartlet and then spray each one with the streusel topping.
6. Put back the tartlets into the Air Fryer and Air-fry the tartlets in batches at 330°F for 15 minutes.
7. Serve and enjoy!!!

Lightning Source UK Ltd.
Milton Keynes UK
UKHW051452050223
416485UK00005B/80

9 781952 504310